Model Engineers' Workshop Projects

Model Engineers' Workshop Projects

Harold Hall

Special Interest Model Books

Special Interest Model Books Ltd.
P.O.Box 327
Poole
Dorset
BH15 2RG
England

Published by Special Interest Model Books Ltd. 2007
Reprinted 2010, 2015, 2017, 2019, 2021

ISBN 978 185486 248 8
Printed and bound in the UK by Martins the Printers

www.specialinterestmodelbooks.co.uk

Contents

Introduction

Owners of home workshops can no doubt be divided into two groups when it comes to making workshop equipment. For some, typically a model engineer involved in constructing a locomotive, making an item of workshop equipment will be a temporary diversion from the main project in hand. Others, like myself, making workshop tooling is almost the sole activity undertaken. In this case many of the projects will be quite substantial, a rotary table, a dividing head, even larger a gear hobbing machine or tool and cutter grinder. These in many cases will get limited use, but will be put on the shelf and looked at with pride saying, "I made that!"

The Items in this book most certainly do not fall into the "I made that!" category. They are though, likely to be hidden in a box somewhere, but brought out frequently to make the task in hand easier than it would have been had they not been made. An important factor in this respect is that most are items that cannot be purchased commercially so making them is the only option should you wish to benefit from having such a device in the workshop. Having made those comments there is

though no reason why a reader should not gain satisfaction from completing any of the items throughout the book.

Whilst predominantly tooling, some fall into a more general group, an auxiliary work bench for example and all can be made in a few hours, some much less, and will repay the time taken many times over.

The contents of this book are all items that I have provided for publication in the Model Engineers' Workshop magazine but unlike most of my published work this book does not go deeply into the methods of manufacture, being more of an ideas book. However, should you like a little more guidance on making the tools featured in this book and have access to past copies of MEW then you could look up the issues in which the items appeared. This book is though a complete rewrite with new photographs and drawings (also having modifications). The original work should therefore only be used as a guide to the manufacturing techniques.

Harold Hall 2007

Chapter 1

Auxiliary Bench

This is the simplest of all the items included and without doubt the one that has repaid my time making it by more times over than any other. It is an auxiliary workbench and took me around 15 minutes to make. I did though have a suitable size piece of ply available for the top, but even if you have to cut the top to size 1 hour should be more than enough.

The bench was initially conceived for holding pieces of sheet steel for cutting using a jig saw, nibbler, etc. This was something I found difficult using my normal bench with it having only one edge available, resulting in clamps and saw wanting to share the same position. The bench, **Photo 1**, is about 450mm square and has a 75mm x 50mm piece of timber screwed onto the under side which is gripped in the bench vice. **Photo 2**, shows

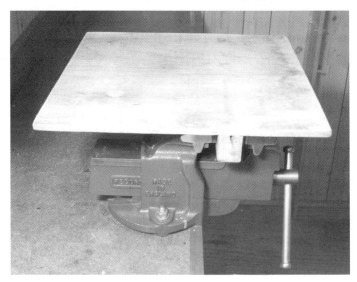

Photo 1 An auxiliary bench with a multitude of uses

Photo 2. Being used to hold a sheet of metal whilst it is being cut using a jig saw.

it being used for it original purpose.

I soon realised that in its elevated position it was also of considerable benefit when marking out, similarly, carrying out delicate assembly work, electronic or mechanical. If you have a small workshop with only limited bench space it will be a worthwhile addition if only to increase your working space, maybe larger may not be a bad idea.

If a long bolt is added to the timber bar this can be gripped in the bench vice and the top tilted to make a small drawing board, **Photo 3**.

File storage

Whilst in a woodworking theme, the method of storing files on the rear of a cupboard door, **Photo 4**, is worth considering. It keeps them in the same place all the time so they are easily found

and by keeping them apart protects their working faces. **Sketch 1** shows the construction in detail. If mounted on a wall rather than on the rear of a door then the lower half could possibly be omitted.

Chuck boards

These were the result of a request from a workshop owner who was beginning to find it difficult to move his lathe chucks to and from the lathe. Additionally, aligning them with the lathe's mandrel.

Photo 5 shows two boards, one for the three jaw and one for the four jaw. These are used on a gap bed lathe and the piece of wood in front is for placing in the gap to prevent the board tipping with the weight of the chuck. Note how the carrying handles pass in front and behind the chuck ensuring they are secure when being carried.

9

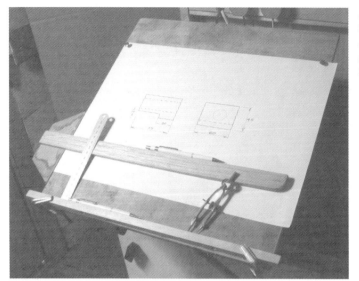

Photo 3 Used tilted it makes a small drawing board for use in the workshop.

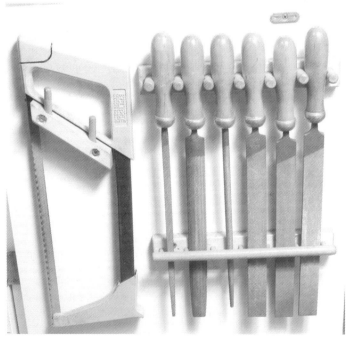

Photo 4 A method of supporting files on the rear of a cupboard door.

Photo 5 These chuck boards make carrying the chucks to and from the lathe an easier operation. Also, whilst on the lathes bed they protect the bed from accidents and holding the chuck at centre height assistin fitting them to the lathe's mandrel.

To make the board place it against the chuck whilst fitted to the lathe and mark its edge with the shape of the chuck. Start chiselling out the shape, frequently checking it for a close fit under the chuck. The ease of screwing the three jaw chuck onto the lathe's mandrel is further enhanced by placing a long length of rod in the chuck and loosely closing the drill chucks jaws onto the other end. This will align the chuck with the mandrel making the process a simple one.

Having started with a woodworking theme, in the next chapter we get down to the real purpose of the book, metalworking!

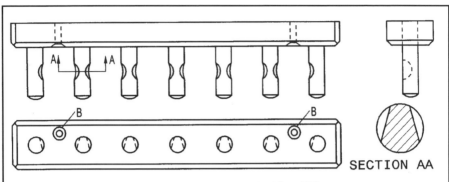

SECTION AA

MATERIAL. WOOD 30 X 18, DOWELS 6mm AND 12mm DIA.

B. DRILL AND COUNTERSINK FOR FIXING SCREWS.

CHOOSE HOLE SIZE IN BASE FOR DOWELS SO THAT THEY CAN BE DRIVEN IN

USE ADHESIVE FOR FIXING FRONT DOWEL ONTO SMALLER DOWELS.

MAKE SMALLER DOWELS LONG ENOUGH TO ENSURE SPACE BETWEEN BASE AND
FRONT DOWEL IS SUFFICIENT TO PERMIT EASY REMOVAL OF FILES.

USE HALF ROUND FILE TO PRODUCE SECTION AS AT AA.

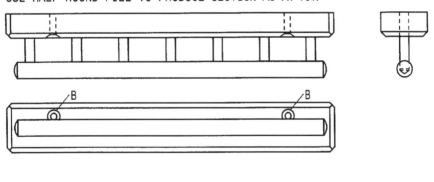

SK1 - FILE STORE

Chapter 2

Tapping Guides

Hand tapping into metal components would at first appear to be a problem free task. This providing the correct tapping size hole has been prepared as an unnecessarily small hole is often the reason for a broken tap!

Attempting the task though it will soon be found not to be as easy as first thought. The main problem is getting the tap to enter in line with the hole's axis. To achieve this it requires the tap to be viewed in two planes, often not that easy. At best the tapped hole may present a problem when the parts are assembled as a tilted screw attempts to pass through a perpendicular clearance hole. With a number of fixings, assembly may only be possible if the clearance holes are increased in size beyond what would be considered acceptable.

This though is not the only problem, especially with small diameter taps. In this case, as the tap enters further into the hole prepared, it will begin to cut more on one side than the other. As a result, smaller

Photo 1 Three typical tapping guides.

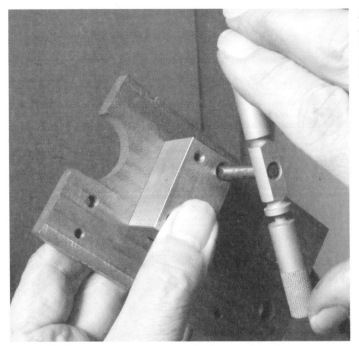

Photo 2. For
smaller sizes
tapping can be
carried out purely
by hand.

size taps are more likely to be broken, even if having the correct tapping hole.

Photo 1 show two forms of tapping guide that, whilst simple, almost eliminates the problems of tapping square. The tap is passed through the appropriate guide and its end located in the hole in the workpiece. With this done, the guide is held onto the workpiece using one hand whilst the other rotates the tap ensuring that the tapped hole is perpendicular to the surface of the component, **Photo 2**.

The process works well providing the tap can be rotated by a single hand, typically a maximum of 2BA, 3/16in or M5. For larger sizes though, the guide will need clamping in place, **Photo 3**. In this, the guide is clamped to the workpiece using a toolmakers clamp which in turn is held in the bench vice.

There will of course be some cases where the nature of the workpiece prevents these guides from being used but for most readers, I would assume they would be suitable for the vast majority of hand tapping carried out. Hardly anywhere else will so little time spent making workshop equipment be repaid so many times over in terms of the quality of the final item. I thoroughly recommend these tapping guides to you!

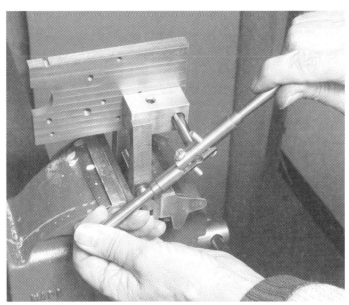

Photo 3. Larger size threads will need the guide to be clamped to the workpiece and held in a bench vice so that both hands are available to turn the tap.

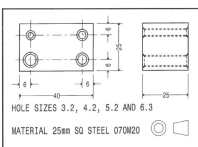

HOLE SIZES 3.2, 4.2, 5.2 AND 6.3

MATERIAL 25mm SQ STEEL 070M20

**METRIC TAPPING GUIDE
SMALL SIZES**

HOLE SIZES 8.3 AND 10.4

MATERIAL 25mm SQ STEEL 070M20

**METRIC TAPPING GUIDE
LARGE SIZES**

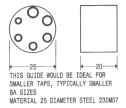

THIS GUIDE WOULD BE IDEAL FOR
SMALLER TAPS, TYPICALLY SMALLER
BA SIZES
MATERIAL 25 DIAMETER STEEL 230M07

SMALLER TAPPING GUIDE

15

Chapter 3

Guided Die Holder

Rather like the problem starting a tap in line with its tapping hole, as mentioned in Chapter 2, similarly, starting a die at an angle will cause the thread to go out of line with the bar on which it is being made, **Photo 1**. This is particularly a problem with long threads. Like the provision of a guide to start a tap, a guide to start a die will overcome the problem.

Two methods are possible, one to make a complete die stock having the provisions for guiding it onto the bar being threaded, Sketch 1, and the other to make guide bushes to use with a standard die stock, **Sketch 2**.

Photo 2 shows a complete die stock for 1in diameter dies, together with guide bushes. Reference to the drawings for this will show that the bushes are just loosely fitted in the die stock with the forward movement of the assembly keeping the bush in place.

Photo 1. A thread that starts out of line will get progressively off axis along the length of the thread.

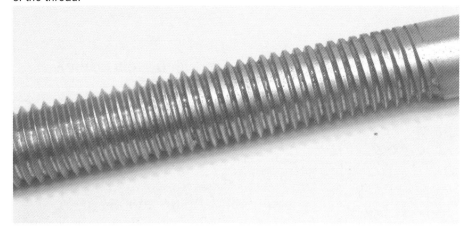

Photo 2. A guided die holder with two guide bushes.

Note though that the workpiece enters the guide first and the die is fitted the opposite way round to normal. However, there is often a sizeable bur on the end of the thread that will prevent the guide bush passing back down the thread, this being more of a problem with larger diameter and coarser threads. However, the bush being loose it can be left at the end of the thread whilst the die is run back towards the start of the thread.

Unfortunately, the method suggested in Sketch 2, has a captive bush and may make removal of the die stock a little difficult on occasions. Also it does not provide access for cleaning the workpiece ahead of the die whilst the thread is being made. Even so, being much easier to make, it may be appropriate for an urgent task or for very infrequent use. I would though suggest that you make guided die stocks for both 13/16in and 1in diameter dies as the system is so much easier to use and produces near perfect results.

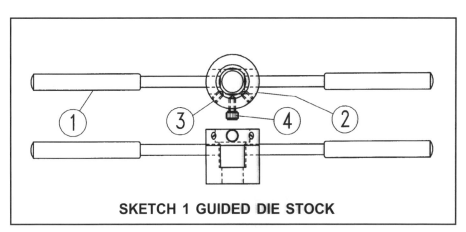

SKETCH 1 GUIDED DIE STOCK

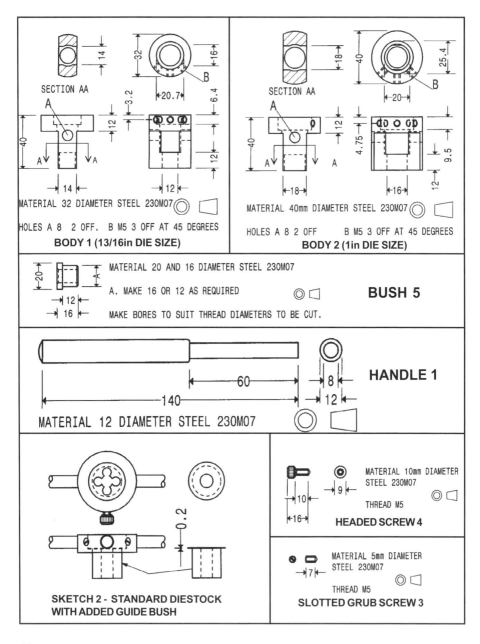

SECTION AA

A

SECTION AA

A

MATERIAL 32 DIAMETER STEEL 230M07

HOLES A 8 2 OFF. B M5 3 OFF AT 45 DEGREES

BODY 1 (13/16in DIE SIZE)

MATERIAL 40mm DIAMETER STEEL 230M07

HOLES A 8 2 OFF   B M5 3 OFF AT 45 DEGREES

BODY 2 (1in DIE SIZE)

MATERIAL 20 AND 16 DIAMETER STEEL 230M07

A. MAKE 16 OR 12 AS REQUIRED

MAKE BORES TO SUIT THREAD DIAMETERS TO BE CUT.

BUSH 5

HANDLE 1

MATERIAL 12 DIAMETER STEEL 230M07

SKETCH 2 - STANDARD DIESTOCK WITH ADDED GUIDE BUSH

MATERIAL 10mm DIAMETER STEEL 230M07

THREAD M5

HEADED SCREW 4

MATERIAL 5mm DIAMETER STEEL 230M07

THREAD M5

SLOTTED GRUB SCREW 3

Chapter 4

Large Tap Wrench

Workshop owners will invariably find themselves at some time working, in size terms, beyond what is the norm for the workshop. Typical of this is the need to tap a hole with a thread much larger than the workshop is geared up for. Having to purchase a tap, maybe two (plug and taper) will be expensive enough for a one off application but the need for a larger tap wrench will only add to project's cost.

Fortunately, making a perfectly adequate wrench is a matter of a few minutes work as the drawing shows. If then it really is a one off job then the screws and materials used can be returned to the raw material stock.

On the other hand, if time is on your side and you wish to make a more professional looking item. **Photo 1** shows how this can be achieved whilst still using the same basic design.

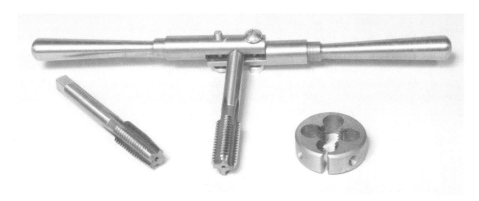

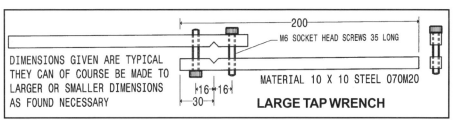

DIMENSIONS GIVEN ARE TYPICAL THEY CAN OF COURSE BE MADE TO LARGER OR SMALLER DIMENSIONS AS FOUND NECESSARY

200

M6 SOCKET HEAD SCREWS 35 LONG

MATERIAL 10 X 10 STEEL 070M20

16 16
30

LARGE TAP WRENCH

Chapter 5

Distance Gauges

The conventional way for establishing a distance using gauges is to use Slip Gauges. These though cover a much wider range than will normally be required in the home workshop, up to a few hundred millimetres depending on how many are stacked together. Of even greater importance, is that they will be much more accurate than will be necessary, typically within 0.00025mm (0.00001in). This all results in an expensive piece of kit.

Like the slip gauges, the distance gauges in this chapter, **Photo 1**, are intended to be stacked and with this done a range of up to 50 mm is possible, again depending on the number of gauges in the stack. Of course you could make longer gauges than I suggest to increase the range. You will not of course be able to produce gauges to the accuracy of the commercial items and my suggestion is to aim to be within + 0.0 - 0.0025mm (0.0001in) Even this level of accuracy will need particular care to achieve.

Working to such tolerances on a lathe is not easy with two aspects being problematical. First, it will need very fine cuts to be taken to finally bring the part to dimension. This not being easy with the leadscrew being calibrated in 0.025 mm

Photo 1 The distance gauges together with outside fingers.

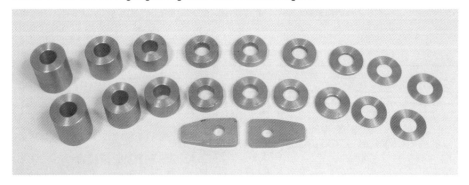

(0.001in) increments when cuts of 0.001 mm (0,00004in) are likely to be required.

When turning outside diameters to precise dimensions it is common practice to set the top slide to an angle of 6°. With this done, traversing the top slide by 0.025 mm will increase the depth of cut by only 0.0025 mm, a ratio of 10: 1. For even greater sensitivity, an angle of 0.6° will give a nominal ratio of 100: 1. However, whilst the top slide's calibration for angles will suffice for 6°, 0.6° will need to be set up differently, more about that later.

Having now got a method of setting a fine depth of cut a suitable tool will be required. It should be obvious that you cannot take a cut 0.001mm deep if the tool is slightly blunt and has a radius of 0.002mm on its cutting edge, it will only rub. Only a freshly honed high speed steel tool can provide such a fine edge. The material used for tipped tools cannot, which in any case are often deliberately supplied slightly radiused to provide strength at the cutting edge.

The gauges in this chapter though require accuracy in terms of length rather than diameter and for this the top slide needs to be set with an angle of just 0.6° between it and the cross slide. To do this, with a DTI mounted on the top slide and reading off the faceplate, adjust the angle so that a variation of 0.5 mm occurs on the indicator reading whilst the top slide is traversed 50mm.

You may have to make temporary arrangements for your top slide to be set at this angle. For my Myford series seven the operating handle fouled the cross slide and had to be replaced with a small round knob. Incidentally, using a between-centres test bar rather than the faceplate,

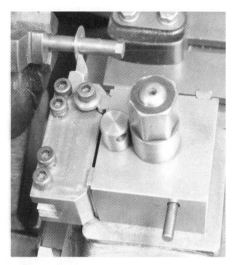

Photo 2 Machining the second face of the distance gauge.

a similar method can be used to set the top slide at 0.6° to the lathe's axis.

Manufacture

With a length of material in the three jaw drill though 6 mm and part off a little longer than the length of the gauge being made. Repeat making at least two of each size. Make a parallel mandrel as per SK1 and use this to hold each gauge in turn for finishing to length. With the first gauge fitted and using a left-hand knife tool face the surface next to the chuck. Do not remove but now with a right hand knife tool fitted, machine the other side precisely to the dimension required **Photo 2**. To do this, use the cross slide, but the angled top slide to place on the required depth of cut. You will increase the depth of cut on one side by feeding the top slide in and feeding it out will increase the cut for the other side. The different length tubes

Left: Photo3.
Finally drilling out
the central hole to
9 mm diameter.

Below: Photo 4
Using a pack of
distance gauges
to set the table
stops on a milling
machine.

shown on SK1 permit the same mandrel to be used for all lengths of gauge.

This process will leave a small unmachined portion at the centre on both sides that can be removed by finally drilling out to 9 mm as per the drawing, **Photo 3**. The gauge is being held for this in the collets detailed in Chapter 11.

Range

The gauges as drawn will provide increments of 0.5 mm up to 50 mm. However, if you would like smaller increments, you could make gauges of 1.1 mm, 1.2 mm, etc. up to 1.9 mm, gauges of 0.1 mm, 0.2 mm, etc. being impractical to make.

Purpose

Having made your distance gauges many uses for them will invariably surface. For me they definitely fit into the category of "why did I not make them earlier?" Only one other item in my workshop beat them into first place in that respect and that is the saddle stop for my lathe. The most used task for the gauges for me is setting the stops on my milling machine, **Photo 4**, similarly the saddle stop on the lathe.

Outside dimensions

A very simple and very worthwhile addition to the gauges would be to add the outside fingers as shown in **Photo 5** for testing outside dimensions. The fingers are seen front of **Photo 1**.

Hole gauges

Whilst in precision mode, you may like to make some hole gauges as seen in **Photo 6**, this time setting the top slide at 0.6° to the axis of the lathe. Otherwise there is little difference between making the hole gauges compared to the distance gauges. The drawing shows that gauges have a

Photo 5 A pack of distance gauges fitted with out side fingers for checking outside dimensions.

small reduced diameter at the start to indicate that the hole is approaching the required diameter. I would though add that in my estimation you will find the distance gauges much more used than the hole gauges, a ratio of at least 20:1 in my workshop.

Photo6 Set of hole gauges, it is though unlikely that you will find these as useful as the distance gauges!

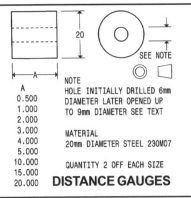

NOTE
HOLE INITIALLY DRILLED 6mm
DIAMETER LATER OPENED UP
TO 9mm DIAMETER SEE TEXT

MATERIAL
20mm DIAMETER STEEL 230M07

QUANTITY 2 OFF EACH SIZE

A
0.500
1.000
2.000
3.000
4.000
5.000
10.000
15.000
20.000

DISTANCE GAUGES

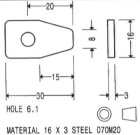

HOLE 6.1

MATERIAL 16 X 3 STEEL 070M20

QUANTITY 2 OFF

OUTSIDE FINGERS

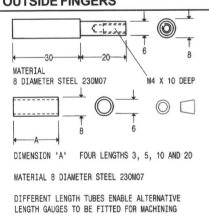

MATERIAL
8 DIAMETER STEEL 230M07   M4 X 10 DEEP

DIMENSION "A"   FOUR LENGTHS 3, 5, 10 AND 20

MATERIAL 8 DIAMETER STEEL 230M07

DIFFERENT LENGTH TUBES ENABLE ALTERNATIVE
LENGTH GAUGES TO BE FITTED FOR MACHINING

PARALELL MANDREL SK1

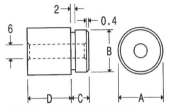

MAKE DIM "B" SMALLER THAN "A" BY
PREFERRED AMOUNT, 0.2mm SUGGESTED

A	C	D
7.000	5	10
8.000	5	11
10.000	6	13
12.000	6	15
14.000	7	17
15.000	7	18
16.000	8	19
20.000	8	23

MATERIAL 230M07 STEEL, DIAMETER TO SUIT

METRIC HOLE GAUGES

THIS SECTION SHOULD TAPER FROM 6.000 WITH AN
INTERNAL ANGLE OF ABOUT 1 DEGREE. THIS WILL
THOUGH DEPEND ON THE ACCURACY OF THE HOLES IN
THE GAUGES WHICH SHOULD PREFERABLY BE REAMED.

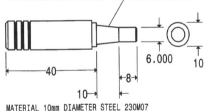

MATERIAL 10mm DIAMETER STEEL 230M07

HANDLE

Chapter 6

Lathe Tool Height Gauge

If you use a lathe tool holder that requires packing to bring the tool to centre height then you will be aware of the trial and error approach necessary. Even if you use a quick

Photo 1 The lathe tool height gauge.

change tool holder its tools will still need setting to centre height, albeit an easier operation. A simple fixed height gauge will ease the problem if the tool is low as the error can be checked using feeler gauges, if high though this will not be possible.

The gauge, **Photo 1**, enables the error to be determined, high or low, and from this suitable changes to the packing height can be determined. For my part, tool holders requiring packing do not deserve the bad press they get from many workshop owners. The answer to the problem is to be organised and have a generous supply of packing already available, cut to the appropriate size and scribed with their thickness. With a good supply of packing thicknesses, setting the tool to the required height should be relatively easy. Remember that packing need not be metal, as hard plastic will do equally well. Because of this, much modern packing, food containers, CD cases, etc. will yield a wide range of shim thicknesses.

The basic principle of the gauge is that the testing surface can be raised or lowered by precise amounts as indicated by the micrometer type barrel. From this reading, the change in packing thickness

required, an increase or decrease, can be determined and the necessary changes made eliminating the need to make trial cuts. On final assembly the gauge is set to read zero at centre height so that the degree of error can be determined, either plus of minus.

The gauge is provided with two testing surfaces enabling top slide, **Photo 2**, and rear toolpost tools, **Photo 3** to be tested

Photo 4 shows the parts ready for final assembly. There should be no problem with this providing that you have ensured that the important diameters, including the threads, are concentric.

The thread's pitch will need to be chosen to suit your workshop's preferred units, Imperial or Metric. For Imperial, a 1/4in x 40 TPI model engineer's thread

Above: Photo 2 The gauge being used for a top slide mounted tool.

Left: Photo 3 For a rear tool post tool the gauge's other testing surface is used. The parting off tool will of course be rotated into the working position after setting.

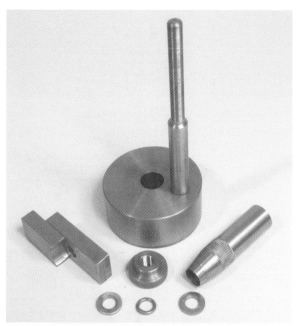

Photo 4 The parts that make up the gauge ready for assembly

will be ideal as this will give 25 one thou (0.001in) divisions, being the same as on an Imperial micrometer. If metric, then an M6 thread having a pitch of 1mm will be the best choice.

The assembly drawing shows that between the lock nut (2) and the arm (3) there is a spring washer with a plain washer on either side. This enables small adjustments to the height using the barrel without having to adjust the nut. Taking a standard spring washer and bending this to increase the set will increase the adjustment available before having to move the nut. The washers enable the arm to be rotated freely.

To calibrate the gauge, place a piece of steel in the chuck and turn a short length accurately to 4.00mm, or 0.100in, depending on the units chosen. Lower the gauge until the arm just contact's the test piece and mark the barrel zero where its calibration coincides with the vertical calibration line on the post. Now lower the barrel by two turns exactly and scribe a line round the post at the end of the barrel. This then is the setting for centre height. The amount by which the zero calibration deviates from the vertical line on the post indicates the amount that the arm is above or below centre height.

Whilst it is always recommended that the tool should be on centre height it is important that it is not above else the front edge will rub, especially for very light cuts and on smaller diameters. For my part, because of this, I always ere on the side of it being below centre, or above for a rear toolpost tool. Having made the gauge this degree of accuracy will be quite easy to achieve!

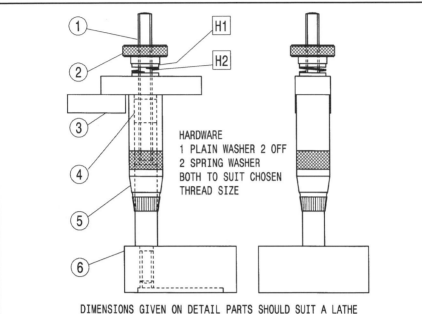

HARDWARE
1 PLAIN WASHER 2 OFF
2 SPRING WASHER
BOTH TO SUIT CHOSEN
THREAD SIZE

DIMENSIONS GIVEN ON DETAIL PARTS SHOULD SUIT A LATHE
CENTRE HEIGHT OF BETWEEN 70mm AND 100mm.
CHANGE PARTS 1 AND OR 6 FOR OTHER CENTRE HEIGHTS.

LATHE TOOL HEIGHT GAUGE

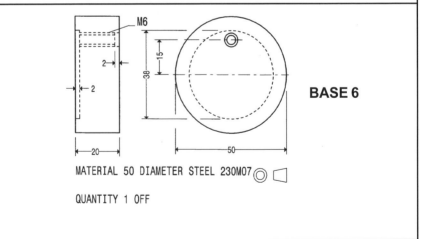

BASE 6

MATERIAL 50 DIAMETER STEEL 230M07

QUANTITY 1 OFF

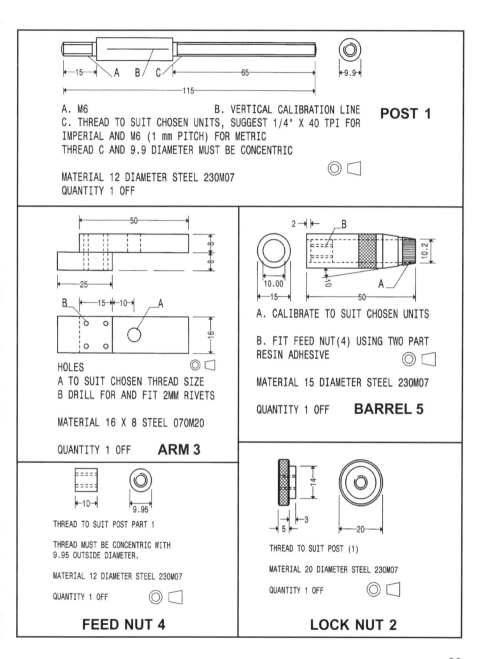

A. M6   B. VERTICAL CALIBRATION LINE

POST 1

C. THREAD TO SUIT CHOSEN UNITS, SUGGEST 1/4" X 40 TPI FOR
IMPERIAL AND M6 (1 mm PITCH) FOR METRIC
THREAD C AND 9.9 DIAMETER MUST BE CONCENTRIC

MATERIAL 12 DIAMETER STEEL 230M07
QUANTITY 1 OFF

HOLES
A TO SUIT CHOSEN THREAD SIZE
B DRILL FOR AND FIT 2MM RIVETS

MATERIAL 16 X 8 STEEL 070M20

QUANTITY 1 OFF   **ARM 3**

A. CALIBRATE TO SUIT CHOSEN UNITS

B. FIT FEED NUT(4) USING TWO PART
RESIN ADHESIVE

MATERIAL 15 DIAMETER STEEL 230M07

QUANTITY 1 OFF   **BARREL 5**

THREAD TO SUIT POST PART 1

THREAD MUST BE CONCENTRIC WITH
9.95 OUTSIDE DIAMETER.

MATERIAL 12 DIAMETER STEEL 230M07

QUANTITY 1 OFF

FEED NUT 4

THREAD TO SUIT POST (1)

MATERIAL 20 DIAMETER STEEL 230M07

QUANTITY 1 OFF

LOCK NUT 2

Chapter 7

Lathe Back Stop

Having to turn even a single part to a precise length can be a minor problem with the normal approach as follows. Make the part ensuring that it is a little on the long side, remove from the chuck and measure the length to determine the amount to be removed. Return the part to the chuck, but obviously it will not be possible to put it back exactly in the same position. Because of this, it will be necessary to bring the tool up to the end of the part before moving the top slide forward

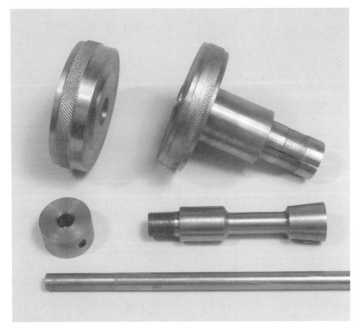

Photo 1 The parts that make up the back stop.

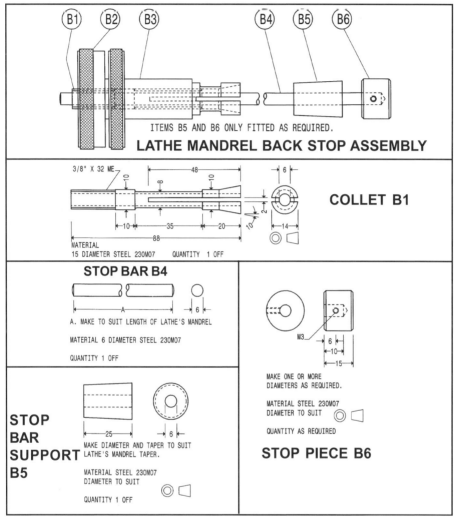

ITEMS B5 AND B6 ONLY FITTED AS REQUIRED.

LATHE MANDREL BACK STOP ASSEMBLY

3/8" X 32 ME

48   6

COLLET B1

10   35   20   14

2

10°

88

MATERIAL
15 DIAMETER STEEL 230M07   QUANTITY 1 OFF

STOP BAR B4

6

A. MAKE TO SUIT LENGTH OF LATHE'S MANDREL

MATERIAL 6 DIAMETER STEEL 230M07

QUANTITY 1 OFF

M3   6
10
15

MAKE ONE OR MORE
DIAMETERS AS REQUIRED.

MATERIAL STEEL 230M07
DIAMETER TO SUIT

QUANTITY AS REQUIRED

STOP PIECE B6

STOP BAR SUPPORT B5

25   6

MAKE DIAMETER AND TAPER TO SUIT
LATHE'S MANDREL TAPER.

MATERIAL STEEL 230M07
DIAMETER TO SUIT

QUANTITY 1 OFF

by the amount to be removed. If however, the part could be returned exactly to the same place the top slide could be just moved forward and the result would be more certain. This is where the benefit of a back stop surfaces as this permits workpieces to be returned to the chuck in exactly the same axial position. However, the real benefit of a back stop is where a batch of identical parts is to be made. In this case the parts will be more accurate and completed in a shorter time.

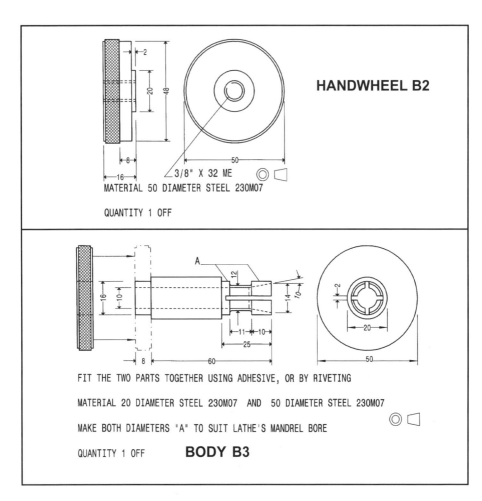

HANDWHEEL B2

3/8" X 32 ME

MATERIAL 50 DIAMETER STEEL 230M07

QUANTITY 1 OFF

FIT THE TWO PARTS TOGETHER USING ADHESIVE, OR BY RIVETING

MATERIAL 20 DIAMETER STEEL 230M07 AND 50 DIAMETER STEEL 230M07

MAKE BOTH DIAMETERS "A" TO SUIT LATHE'S MANDREL BORE

QUANTITY 1 OFF   **BODY B3**

The Stop piece (B6) is also useful to support a part held in the three-jaw chuck but where only a short length is available for gripping. Typically, a part whose thickness is thin compared to its length

When in use the inner collet (B1) is pulled into the body (B3) by the Handwheel (B2) closing the inner collet onto the Stop bar (B4) but simultaneously expanding the main body into the bore of the lathe's mandrel, thereby firmly holding them in place. The drawings suit a lathe with a mandrel bore of 5/8in for other bores you will need to change some dimensions.

Manufacture is straightforward and needs no comment. **Photo 1** shows the parts, except for the stop bar support (B5), that make up the device.

Chapter 8

Tailstock Die Holders

The subject in this paragraph is certainly one that can be purchased commercially and relatively cheaply. If this is done though, it is likely that a single one will be acquired and the die changed each time a change of thread is required. The holders in this chapter are though very simple to make, especially if made in quantity, and therefor suggest one for each regularly used thread size would be a good idea. This would probably make it financially worthwhile to make them in the shop rather than purchase. In either case you will have to make the tailstock adapter for supporting the holders. Also, the commercial holders will need drilling for Tommy bar operation as they are intended for machine rather than manual operation.

Photo1 Two sizes of die stock 13/16in and 1in fitted with dies for M3 through to M10. Two holders without dies are for use with dies used only occasionally.

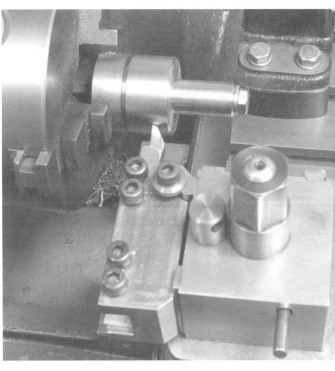

Photo 2 Machining the shank and outer diameter whilst held on a stub mandrel.

Photo 1 shows a set of holders housing M3, M4, M5, M6, M8 and M10 together with two spares for occasional use with other sizes, Model Engineers 40 TPI typically. The photograph also shows an adapter having a Number 2 Morse taper shank. If you do not want to be involved in turning a taper shank then making one with a short parallel portion for holding in the drill chuck would be another approach, though not ideal

Manufacture

The essential requirement for these holders is that the bore for the die and the shank should be concentric. The easiest way of achieving this is to make the bore

and to turn the shank with a left-hand knif tool, doing this without removing the pa from the chuck. This though will leave small stub of steel in the chuck after partin off that may not find a use. The followin method will avoid any wastage of materia

Cut the required number of pieces c steel, just longer than the finished item Mount in the chuck and face the first enc Also commence to machine the shank bu leaving it about 1 mm larger on diamete and shorter on length, remove, turn en on end, refit. Now, face the other end an drill through with the drill size quoted followed by making the bore to house th die. Repeat for as many holders as yo decide to make.

Photo 3 You do not need an expensive dividing head for much of the work in the home workshop. This one is perfectly adequate for the Tommy bar and grub screw holes. The holder is being held on the same stub mandrel as was used for turning the shank.

Place a short piece of steel in the chuck and turn a short stub mandrel a close fit in the bore for holding the die. Make the stub mandrel, say 3 mm long, allowing the flange to mate with the end of the holder. Drill and tap M6. Do not remove until all the holders have been completed. If you work on the larger holders first, the stub can then be reduced for use with the smaller holders.

Fit the first holder and finish turn the shank to the appropriate diameter and length and skim the outer diameter, **Photo 2**. This process ensures that both the shank and die seat are concentric. Repeat for the remaining holders

The remaining operations need no comment though you may be interested in my set up for drilling the Tommy bar holes, **Photo 3**. Note that this uses the same mandrel for holding the parts for drilling whilst still fitted in the chuck.

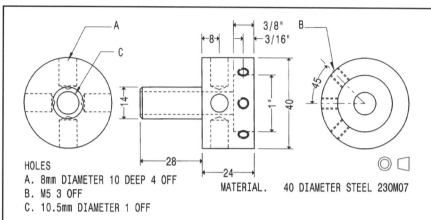

HOLES
A. 8mm DIAMETER 10 DEEP 4 OFF
B. M5 3 OFF
C. 10.5mm DIAMETER 1 OFF

MATERIAL.   40 DIAMETER STEEL 230M07

1 INCH DIE HOLDER

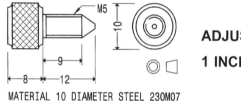

ADJUSTER SCREW

1 INCH DIE HOLDER

MATERIAL 10 DIAMETER STEEL 230M07

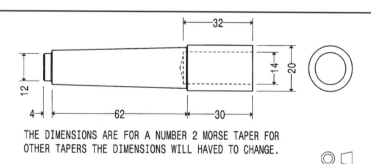

THE DIMENSIONS ARE FOR A NUMBER 2 MORSE TAPER FOR
OTHER TAPERS THE DIMENSIONS WILL HAVED TO CHANGE.

MATERIAL   20 DIAMETER STEEL 230M07

TAILSTOCK DIE HOLDER SUPPORT

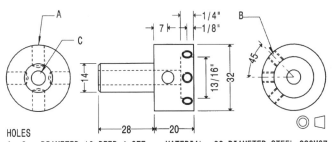

HOLES
A. 6mm DIAMETER 10 DEEP 4 OFF   MATERIAL 32 DIAMETER STEEL 230M07
B. M5 3 OFF
C. 7mm DIAMETER 1 OFF

13/16 INCH DIE HOLDER

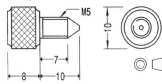

ADJUSTER SCREW
13/16 INCH DIE
HOLDER

MATERIAL 10 DIAMETER STEEL 230M07

Chapter 9

Face Plate and Angle Plate Clamps

The main problem with holding workpieces, both on the faceplate and angle plate, is their small size and limited number of fixing slots. Their small size in particular makes the clamps used on the milling machine table invariably too large for these situations. The clamps in this chapter seek to overcome this problem which takes a fresh look at the method to use. The system will be described in terms of its use on the faceplate where there are particular considerations, when used on the angle plate the method will be much the same though less demanding.

Photo 1 A range of parts that make up the clamping system. However, for maximum benefit more of each part should be made than shown.

Photo 2 A typical application for the clamping system

A single clamping set-up will comprise a clamp bar with a central clamping stud and with one end holding the component whilst the other rests on a packing piece of some form. This needs to be just higher than the component. Whilst this is perfectly acceptable on the milling machine table it has safety considerations when used on the faceplate. In this case, the rotation of the faceplate will be attempting to throw out the packing and if not fully secure for some reason could be potentially very dangerous. Because of this, the clamps in this chapter have been designed to be both compact, and for the packing to be captive.

Sketch 1 illustrates the basic design whilst **Photo 1** shows a range of typical parts. As the packing is tapped it shows that the packing and clamp screw are both captive prior to clamping the workpiece. This is a major advantage when fixing the first clamp as with both the packing and the clamp screw being firmly fixed there is still one hand to hold the workpiece and one to tighten the clamp screw nut. After having fixed the component in place with two or more clamps, individual clamps and packing pieces can easily be loosened to move them into better positions.

As the packing has to be just higher than the workpiece a large number of different height packing pieces would be required. To minimise this, height increasing bushes are made in a range of heights so that they can be used in combinations and with the packing pieces, also made in a few heights, to cover a range dimensions with the minimum number of parts, SK 2 illustrates this. The height increasing bushes have clearance holes.

As the number of fixing slots is limited making it difficult to get the clamping screw in precisely the best place in some cases, additional flexibility is achieved by a second hole in the packing pieces and height increasing bushes. This set up is seen in SK 3. This though results in the clamping screw being nearer the packing than the workpiece, which is not ideal. The set up should therefor only be used where that in SK 1 is not possible, preferably then only as a back up where some clamps as per SK 1 are also being used. **Photo 2** shows a typical application where the parts are being used on the faceplate.

With a suitable screw added, the packing pieces would also make useful mini jacks, **Photo 3**. These could have uses in a

Photo 3 With a screw added a packing piece makes a useful mini jack.

wide range of situations. The clamp plates could also be used alone in conventional clamping set-ups on the milling machine.

All the parts are simple to make and would benefit from generous quantities being made. In this respect, it is easier to make an extra one or two of an item at the initial stage than going back and making more later. Some thoughts in terms of production methods would help to speed up their manufacture.

To gain maximum benefit from using these clamps on the faceplate, why not make the Faceplate Balancing Fixture described in Chapter 13.

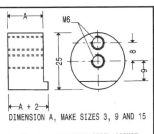

DIMENSION A, MAKE SIZES 3, 9 AND 15

MATERIAL 25 DIAMETER STEEL 230M07

QTY 3 OFF EACH SIZE MINIMUM ◎ ◁

PACKING PIECES

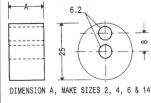

DIMENSION A, MAKE SIZES 2, 4, 6 & 14

MATERIAL 25 DIAMETER STEEL 230M07

QTY 3 OFF EACH SIZE MINIMUM ◎ ◁

HEIGHT INCREASING BUSH

MATERIAL
20 DIAMETER STEEL 230M07

QUANTITY 8 MINIMUM

CLAMP SCREW WASHER

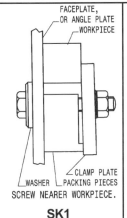

SCREW NEARER WORKPIECE.

SK1

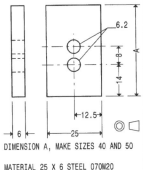

DIMENSION A, MAKE SIZES 40 AND 50

MATERIAL 25 X 6 STEEL 070M20

QTY 4 OFF EACH SIZE MINIMUM

CLAMP PLATES

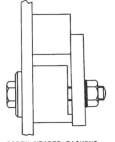

MATERIAL 30 DIAMETER STEEL 230M07

QUANTITY AS REQUIRED ◎ ◁

WIDE SLOT WASHER

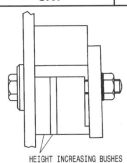

HEIGHT INCREASING BUSHES

HEIGHT INCREASING WASHERS BEING USED SK2

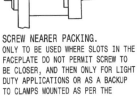

SCREW NEARER PACKING.
ONLY TO BE USED WHERE SLOTS IN THE
FACEPLATE DO NOT PERMIT SCREW TO
BE CLOSER, AND THEN ONLY FOR LIGHT
DUTY APPLICATIONS OR AS A BACKUP
TO CLAMPS MOUNTED AS PER THE
PREFERED METHOD.

NON-PREFERRED METHOD SK3

Chapter 10

Lathe Collets

Commercially available collets are now so relatively cheap that making collets, other than as an interesting project, may seem pointless. However, holders for the collets in the ER series mostly come with Morse, or other, taper shank and do not allow bar material to pass through them. They are therefore only suitable for short workpieces although there are now signs of this shortcoming being addressed by the tool suppliers. Even so, I am sure there will be some who will say that there is no need to make collets in view of them being readily available, a comment with which I have some sympathy. I have thought included this chapter, as some of the item are common with the thin piece collets in Chapter 11, items that to my knowledge are not readily available commercially.

The conventional collets with holder

Photo 1 Conventional collets and collet body.

Photo 2   Individual jaws enable small square sections to be held in round collets.

an be seen in **Photo 1** and reference to ‑hapter 11, **Photo 2**, shows that both ystems use the same body that mounts ꞵ the lathe spindle nose

As I explained in the Introduction it is ot my intention to go deeply into ᴝanufacturing techniques for items in this ᴼok and this item is one where the reader hould have no problem if conversant with ᴀsic turning methods. Concentricity is the ᴼost vital consideration and the following ᴇquence would be worth following.

Make sufficient collet blanks producing ᴛ this stage just the 16mm bore, the rear ᴀrallel portions and the 20° taper. Drill ᴛrough 3.5 mm and part off. If you carry out ᴉis stage using a fixed steady you will not ᴫd up with a small stub after making each ᴫe. Leave the top slide set at 20°!

Now fit a short length of say 25 mm ᴉameter steel in the three jaw and bore ᴇ9.00 mm diameter 3 mm deep, drill and

tap the centre M3, do not remove from the chuck. This can then be used to hold each collet in turn to produce the 16mm diameter and the 10° front face. Do not set the top slide at 10° but set the knife tool round at this angle as illustrated in the drawing showing this set up. Make the angled face in stages taking only a very light finishing cut over the complete width.

Make the collet closing ring but again do not move the top slide from its 20° position but finally set the boring tool round to produce the 10° angle using its front face. As with the collet this face will have to be machined with caution, especially in this case due to the overhang of the boring tool. Whilst it is essential that the 20° angle is the same for both the collet and the collet body the 10° is not so important, hence the method proposed

The final major process is to make the lathe collet body making the 19.00mm

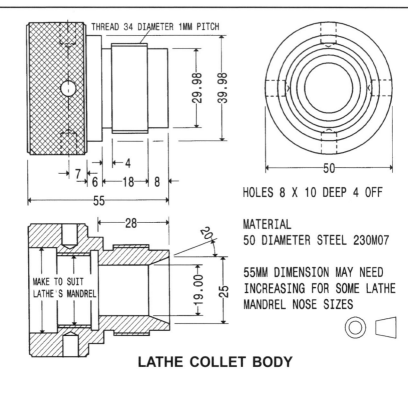

THREAD 34 DIAMETER 1MM PITCH

29.98

39.98

4

7

6 ←18→ 8

55

HOLES 8 X 10 DEEP 4 OFF

MATERIAL
50 DIAMETER STEEL 230M07

55MM DIMENSION MAY NEED
INCREASING FOR SOME LATHE
MANDREL NOSE SIZES

28

20°

19.00

25

MAKE TO SUIT
LATHE'S MANDREL

50

LATHE COLLET BODY

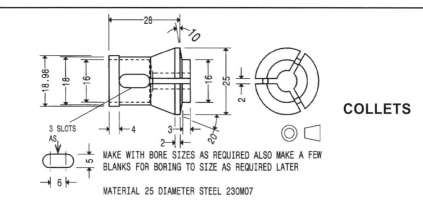

28

10

18.98

18

16

16

25

2

3 SLOTS
AS

4

3

2

20°

5

6

MAKE WITH BORE SIZES AS REQUIRED ALSO MAKE A FEW
BLANKS FOR BORING TO SIZE AS REQUIRED LATER

MATERIAL 25 DIAMETER STEEL 230M07

COLLETS

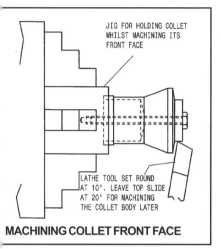

JIG FOR HOLDING COLLET
WHILST MACHINING ITS
FRONT FACE

LATHE TOOL SET ROUND
AT 10°. LEAVE TOP SLIDE
AT 20° FOR MACHINING
THE COLLET BODY LATER

MACHINING COLLET FRONT FACE

ore and the 20° face last. This will ensure
hat they are running perfectly true for boring
he collets. You will of course have to use
an inverted boring bar, machining on the
ear face for producing the angle. Fit the
losing ring and finish its outer surfaces.

Now fit each collet in turn and bore, not
rill, to the sizes required. Slit the collets,
rill holes for Tommy bars, etc. and the job
s done. The jig made for holding the collets
vhile turning the front face can also be used
or holding them whilst they are being slit.

Collets for square materials

Providing you have a collet system for your
athe, be it that above or some other, the
ollets in this chapter will give you the
nswer to a very difficult problem. That is,
ow to hold small square bar, particularly
ery small, say 3mm.

Making a complete collet for round
naterial is quite a lengthy task, but if
quare, very lengthy, as a broach would
ave to be made to produce the square.
here would then still be the problem of

ensuring that it was concentric.

The idea proposed for using four individual
jaws in an existing round collet overcomes the
problem with ease and the manufacturing time
will be no more than half an hour.

Take four lengths of square material of
suitable size and length and hold then in the
four jaw separating them with thin card as
SK1 shows. Turn a length, say 30mm for
smaller sizes, to fit the chosen round collet.
Then turn a further 3mm to a larger diameter
to eventually produce a head and part off at
this length. When making the jaws to this
stage it would be a good idea to make a few
additional sets of jaws for eventual use as
other square sizes need to be held.

Now all that is needed is to produce a
flat on the corners that will eventually grip
the square material. For larger sizes doing
this on the milling machine is probably
best but for smaller sizes filing it whilst
held in the vice will not be difficult. Having
worked out the dimension, just place a
micrometer across the curved surface onto
the flat and at points along the length of
the jaw to check progress. SK2 details how
the required dimension can be arrived at.
Do not assume that you just remove half
the width of the square, as this does not
take into account the width of the space
between the individual jaws when in use

Photo 2 shows a set of jaws in a collet
chuck holding a small square section and
separately two sets of jaws made for other
sizes. Whilst as a last resort the four jaw
chuck could be used the collet system will
win hands down when making very small
parts in large numbers, square nuts for a
model horse drawn cart for example. Also,
running the collet at a very high speed for
the task will be much more pleasant than
running a large four jaw at such speeds.

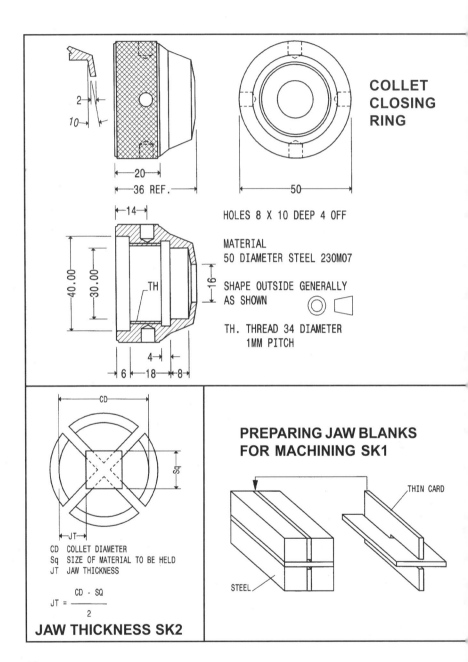

COLLET CLOSING RING

HOLES 8 X 10 DEEP 4 OFF

MATERIAL
50 DIAMETER STEEL 230M07

SHAPE OUTSIDE GENERALLY
AS SHOWN

TH. THREAD 34 DIAMETER
1MM PITCH

CD COLLET DIAMETER
Sq SIZE OF MATERIAL TO BE HELD
JT JAW THICKNESS

$$JT = \frac{CD - SQ}{2}$$

JAW THICKNESS SK2

PREPARING JAW BLANKS FOR MACHINING SK1

THIN CARD

STEEL

Chapter 11

Thin Piece Collets

For most, there will come a time when a thin piece collet will be an essential item for a particular task in hand as often there is no acceptable alternative. The workshop owner may of course attempt to get by with a temporary solution such as those shown in **Photo 1** and which are used in the three of four jaw chuck. They will though fall short of the ideal in terms of accuracy and security of the hold provided.

The collets described in this chapter

Photo 1 Two thin piece collets for use in the three jaw chuck. These are not idea but are an option for a one off application.

seek to provide a better solution and are shown in **Photo 2**, which includes the parts, excluding the draw bar, that make up the system. These collets will hold material up to 28 mm diameter. From this, and **Photo 1** in Chapter 10 it can be seen that both collet systems use the same body. However, if you are just making this part of the system, only the body will require making plus the handwheel and draw bar. Even for this it will not be necessary to produce the external threads, etc. on the body

As **Photo 2** shows, make a few collets still left long for repeated boring to sizes required as later projects dictate. You can though make at this stage one to take your most common sizes as seen, centre of the photograph

The collets with removable jaws, **Photo 3**, are more complex but will allow larger diameters to be machined. Again make some spare jaws (left of the photograph) for possible boring at other diameters at a later date. Of course, being soft, even the already bored collets can be re-machined for other diameters. With this and the other thin piece collets, it will be necessary to make a close fitting plug (centre of Photo 2) to go into the bore to

Photo 2 The parts that make up the system at the smaller diameters. There is also a draw bar that is not shown in the photograph.

stop the slots closing when subsequently boring out to additional or new diameters. This is best made at the same time as the collets are made.

The thin piece collet system is particularly useful as photograph 3 in Chapter 5 illustrates. In this a distance gauge, 2.0 mm thick, is having a hole drilled

Photo 3 A collet for larger diameters, also a spare jaw for possible future use.

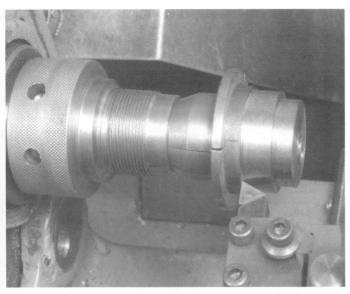

Photo 4 This photograph shows that these collets can be used at longer lengths. Their use really being where only a small length of the workpiece is available for gripping in the chuck

to a larger size but was similarly used down to 0.5 mm thick, something that would be quite difficult by any other means.

Photo 4 shows the removable jaw collet in use and illustrates that the term 'thin piece collet' is not exactly accurate. They are mainly for use in a situation where only a small portion of the workpiece is available to be gripped in the chuck or collet. Of course, the further the item projects from the collet the more cautious one must be in terms of depth of cut and feed rate. I have though taken a cut of 3mm wide at 40mm diameter and 25mm from the collet, with a sharp tool, and a delicate feed, I must admit

The part being held though must have a square corner, in which case a depth of bore of 1 mm in the collet should suffice. For less precise workpieces and or the need to work some distance from the collet, say more than the part's diameter, then a bore depth of 2mm would be a wise precaution

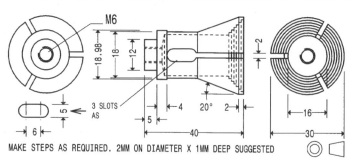

MAKE STEPS AS REQUIRED. 2MM ON DIAMETER X 1MM DEEP SUGGESTED

MATERIAL 30 DIAMETER STEEL 230M07   **STEPPED COLLET**

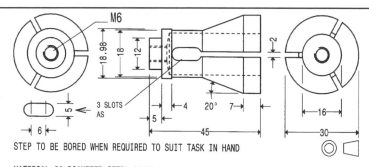

STEP TO BE BORED WHEN REQUIRED TO SUIT TASK IN HAND

MATERIAL 30 DIAMETER STEEL 230M07

GENERAL PURPOSE COLLET

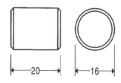

PLUG

TO BE A CLOSE FIT IN THE
GENERAL PURPOSE COLLET BORE

USED TO PREVENT COLLET
CLOSING WHEN SUBSEQUENTLY
BORED TO SUIT TASK IN HAND

MATERIAL 20 DIAMETER
STEEL 230M07

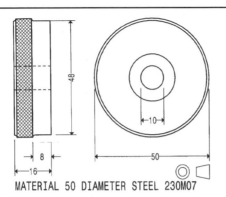

HANDWHEEL

MATERIAL 50 DIAMETER STEEL 230M07

USE TWO PART RESIN ADHESIVE TO FIX
HANDWHEEL TO HANDWHEEL BUSH

QUANTITY 1 OFF

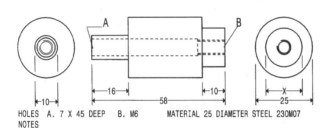

HOLES A. 7 X 45 DEEP   B. M6   MATERIAL 25 DIAMETER STEEL 230M07
NOTES

X. TO BE A FREE FIT IN THE LATHE'S MANDREL BORE

QUANTITY 1 OFF   **HANDWHEEL BUSH**

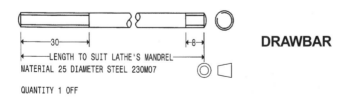

DRAWBAR

LENGTH TO SUIT LATHE'S MANDREL
MATERIAL 25 DIAMETER STEEL 230M07

QUANTITY 1 OFF

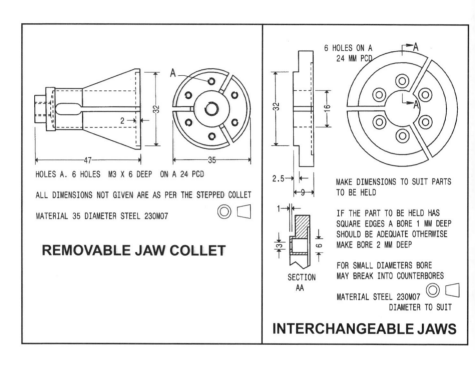

HOLES A. 6 HOLES M3 X 6 DEEP ON A 24 PCD

ALL DIMENSIONS NOT GIVEN ARE AS PER THE STEPPED COLLET

MATERIAL 35 DIAMETER STEEL 230M07

REMOVABLE JAW COLLET

6 HOLES ON A
24 MM PCD

SECTION
AA

MAKE DIMENSIONS TO SUIT PARTS
TO BE HELD

IF THE PART TO BE HELD HAS
SQUARE EDGES A BORE 1 MM DEEP
SHOULD BE ADEQUATE OTHERWISE
MAKE BORE 2 MM DEEP

FOR SMALL DIAMETERS BORE
MAY BREAK INTO COUNTERBORES

MATERIAL STEEL 230M07
DIAMETER TO SUIT

INTERCHANGEABLE JAWS

Chapter 12

Dial Test Indicator Accessories

The term "Dial test indicator Accessories" greatly understates the possibilities with the subject of this chapter. As will be seen it can satisfy a wide range of requirements and is as a result the largest project in the book. However, it is by no means the most complex. Central to the equipment is the flexible joint and whilst this is available commercially most of the other items will have to be shop made.

Flexible joints

Photo 1 shows the full range of parts though the reader will only have to make

Photo 1 The full range of parts that make up the kit. You will though need more of the flexible joints and bars than are shown.

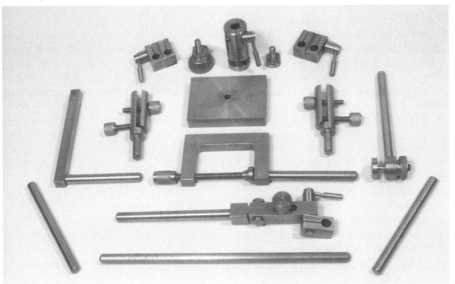

Photo 2 A set up permanently stored for immediate use on the lathe.

those items that are likely to be useful in the workshop where they are to be used. However, do make at least 8 flexible joints (AS1) as you may be surprised just how many you will use, especially if you keep some of the assemblies ready made up for use, that in **Photo 2** being typical. In this a DTI is prepared for use on the lathe being coupled up to a holder in my quick-change system. The indicator itself can of course be rapidly removed for use elsewhere but still leaving the bulk of the set up intact

Some DTI's have mounting barrels that are smaller than the 8mm diameter of the bars so you may need some joints with one half having a smaller hole. It may even be a good idea to make a few without a

hole so that it will be easy at a later date to make an arm clamp (F1) with a different hole size to those available. As the joints can easily be dismantled it will be possible to mix and match diameters as required. Note that the taper bit, SK1, is for making the tapered counterbore in each half of the flexible joint.

Also, you will need a range of arm (A1) lengths and would suggest at least three of each size.

Mounts

Having made your joints and arms they will be of little use without the means of mounting them and it is here where the absence of easily available commercial

54

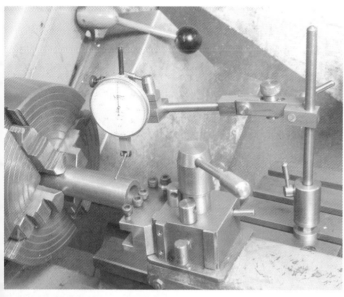

Left: Photo 3 A set up mounted off the lathes cross slide for testing the concentricity of the part in the chuck. Note the use of the adjustable arm that enables the amount of contact with the workpiece to be set.
Below: Photo 4 A permanently fitted mount, under the down feed stop bracket, is ideal for locating a dial test indicator, etc.

items makes it necessary to manufacture the provisions in the workshop. **Photo 3** shows how a dial test indicator can be firmly mounted on the lathes cross slide using its T slots. T slots are likely to be larger on other machines so that more than one size of T bolt will be required. These are parts M1, M2, M3 and M4, you may however need to change the sizes of M2 and M3 to suit your machines. The large washer is to support the General Purpose Mount (M1) when used with a large T slot.

Mostly, when used on a milling machine, the dial requires to remain stationary whilst the table moves. This requires the assembly to be mounted off a non-moving part of the machine, **Photo 4** showing a possible solution. In this, the mount (M5), is mounted off the down feed stop bracket where it can be left permanently

As an alternative to using the T slot

Right: Photo 5 Using a G clamp to hold a DTI.

Below: Photo 6 A base plate enables assemblies to be free standing.

mounting method on the lathe, the right angle mount (M7) could be used directly off the top slide or even permanently mounted into a quick change tool holder for rapid use as was seen in **Photo 2**. Another rapid method of mounting and removing an assembly is to use the G clamp mount, **Photo 5**. This comprises G1, G2, G3 and G4. The Vee Pad (G5) is used when mounting it onto a round support as in the photograph.

Sometimes it is useful to be able to use the system free standing, **Photo 6**. For this it will be necessary to make the base (B1). This simple component opens up many more possibilities. **Photo 7** shows it as a holder for a magnifying glass for intricate work. **Photo 8** shows it being used as an instrument makers vice, very useful for those who do modelling or other tasks in the smallest scales. If you are into electronics then using it for

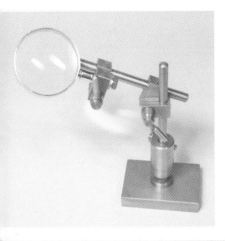

assembling **Photo 9** and soldering **Photo 10** would be very well worthwhile.

Photo's 8, 9, 10 and 11 are seen using the clamp C1/C2. These use two screws for securing the item being held, in the same way as a standard toolmakers clamp. **Photo 11** shows one being used for holding a machine guard.

Another very useful addition is the adjustable arm (AS2) as seen in Photo 3. This is a little more complex than other items but the only crucial item is that items A5 and A7 are adjusted so that there is no back lash present. When set, it is locked using setscrew part H1.

Above left: Photo 7 A magnifying lens stand.

Left: Photo 8 Being used as an instrument makers vice for delicate work.

57

Right and Below:
Photos 9 and 10
Being used for
electronic
assembly.

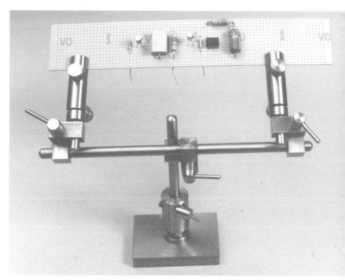

There are a few other items, locking screws, etc. that have not had a mention. However, the photographs together with the drawings should make their use obvious. No doubt, the reader will find other useful applications, perhaps even designing other parts to augment the system

Whilst some items in the system find only occasional use the basic kit fo mounting a dial test indicator typically gets very frequent use and must rate in my top three workshop items that I have made The others being the distance gauges (Chapter 5) and my saddle stop for my lathe.

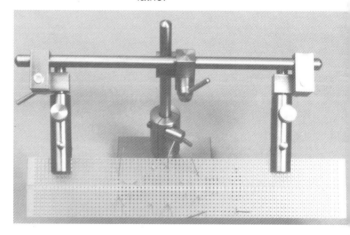

Photo 11 Holding a light weight machine guard.

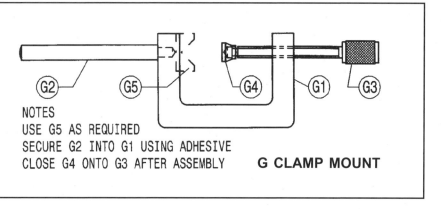

NOTES
USE G5 AS REQUIRED
SECURE G2 INTO G1 USING ADHESIVE
CLOSE G4 ONTO G3 AFTER ASSEMBLY

G CLAMP MOUNT

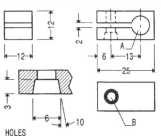

HOLES
A. 8 MM TO SUIT BARS, OTHER DIAMETER
   TO SUIT DTI MOUNTS, ETC. AS
   REQUIRED
B. 4.2

MATERIAL 12 MM SQ STEEL 070M20

QTY MAKE 12 OFF HOLE B 8 MM DIAMETER
   OTHERS AS REQUIRED.

ARM CLAMP F1

A. MAKE IN VARIOUS LENGTHS.
   SUGGESTED, 50, 100, 150 AND 200

MATERIAL 8 DIAMETER STEEL 230M07

QUANTITY MINIMUM 4 OFF 50 AND 100 LENGTHS
AND 2 OFF 150 AND 200 LENGTHS.

ARMS A1

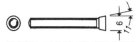

MATERIAL M4 X 30 HEX HEAD SCREW

QUANTITY SUFFICIENT FOR THE
NUMBER OF CLAMPS MADE

CLAMP SCREW F3

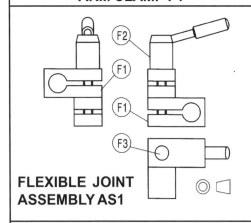

FLEXIBLE JOINT
ASSEMBLY AS1

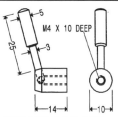

SHAPE GENERALLY AS SHOWN
USE ADHESIVE TO FIX ARM

MATERIAL
   10 DIAMETER STEEL 230M07
   5 DIAMETER STEEL 230M07

QUANTITY AS REQUIRED

CLAMPING NUT F2

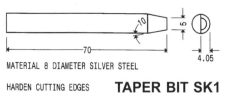

MATERIAL 8 DIAMETER SILVER STEEL

HARDEN CUTTING EDGES   **TAPER BIT SK1**

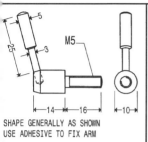

SHAPE GENERALLY AS SHOWN
USE ADHESIVE TO FIX ARM

MATERIAL 10 DIAMETER STEEL 230M07
5 DIAMETER STEEL 230M07

QUANTITY AS REQUIRED

MOUNT CLAMPING SCREW M6

M5

MAKE HEXAGON TO SUIT
PREFERRED SPANNER

SECTION AA
HOLE SIZES
A. 8
B. 4.5
C. M4
D. M6 X 15 DEEP
MATERIAL 25 DIAMETER STEEL 230M07

QUANTITY MAKE NUMBER REQUIRED

GENERAL PURPOSE MOUNT M1

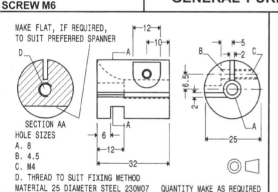

MAKE FLAT, IF REQUIRED,
TO SUIT PREFERRED SPANNER

SECTION AA
HOLE SIZES
A. 8
B. 4.5
C. M4
D. THREAD TO SUIT FIXING METHOD
MATERIAL 25 DIAMETER STEEL 230M07   QUANTITY MAKE AS REQUIRED

FIXED MOUNT M5

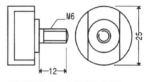

M6

FOR USING IN LARGE TEE SLOTS
TYPICALLY MILLING MACHINE SLIDES

MAKE OTHER SIZES TO SUIT

MATERIAL
25 DIAMETER STEEL 230M07

QUANTITY AS REQUIRED

LARGE TEE BOLT M3

SMALL TEE BOLT M2

M6

FOR USING IN SMALL TEE SLOTS
TYPICALLY LATHE CROSS SLIDES

MAKE OTHER SIZES TO SUIT

MATERIAL
20 DIAMETER STEEL 230M07

QUANTITY AS REQUIRED

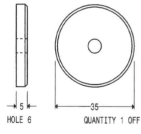

HOLE 6   QUANTITY 1 OFF

MATERIAL 35 DIAMETER STEEL 230M07

FOR USE ON WIDE TEE SLOTS

MOUNT SUPPORT WASHER M4

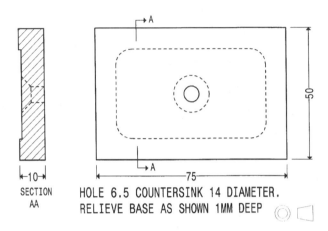

10

SECTION
AA

HOLE 6.5 COUNTERSINK 14 DIAMETER.
RELIEVE BASE AS SHOWN 1MM DEEP

75

50

MATERIAL 50 X 10 STEEL 070M20   QUANTITY 1 OFF

BASE B1

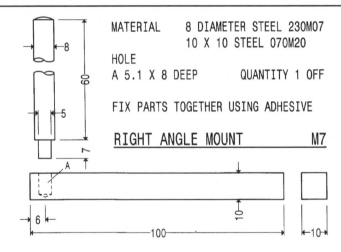

MATERIAL   8 DIAMETER STEEL 230M07
             10 X 10 STEEL 070M20

HOLE
A 5.1 X 8 DEEP   QUANTITY 1 OFF

FIX PARTS TOGETHER USING ADHESIVE

RIGHT ANGLE MOUNT   M7

8

60

5

7

A

6

100

10

10

RIGHT ANGLE MOUNT M7

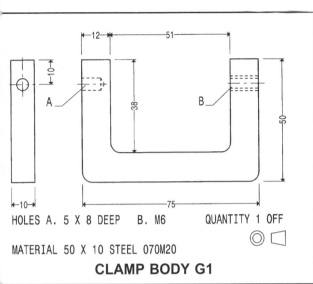

HOLES A. 5 X 8 DEEP   B. M6   QUANTITY 1 OFF

MATERIAL 50 X 10 STEEL 070M20

CLAMP BODY G1

CLAMP SCREW PAD G4

MATERIAL
10 DIAMETER STEEL 230M07

SHAPE GENERALLY AS DRAWING

QUANTITY 1 OFF

MATERIAL 8 DIAMETER STEEL 230M07   QUANTITY 1 OFF

CLAMP ARM G2

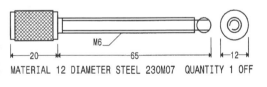

M6

MATERIAL 12 DIAMETER STEEL 230M07   QUANTITY 1 OFF

CLAMP SCREW G3

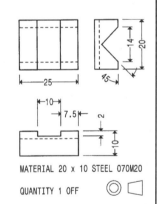

MATERIAL 20 x 10 STEEL 070M20

QUANTITY 1 OFF

G CLAMP MOUNT VEE BLOCK G5

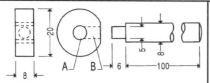

HOLES A 6.5   B 5.1   QUANTITY 1 OFF

MATERIAL 20 DIAMETER STEEL 230M07
         8 DIAMETER STEEL 230M07

FIX PARTS TOGETHER USING ADHESIVE.

DIAL INDICATOR ARM D1

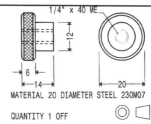

MATERIAL 20 DIAMETER STEEL 230M07

QUANTITY 1 OFF

DIAL INDICATOR NUT D2

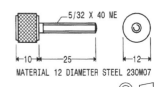

MATERIAL 12 DIAMETER STEEL 230M07

QUANTITY 4 OFF

CLAMP SCREW C2

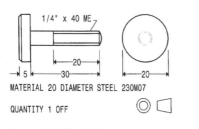

MATERIAL 20 DIAMETER STEEL 230M07

QUANTITY 1 OFF

DIAL INDICATOR SCREW D2

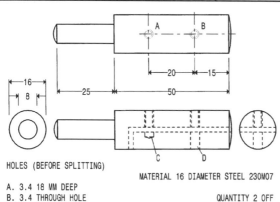

HOLES (BEFORE SPLITTING)

MATERIAL 16 DIAMETER STEEL 230M07

A. 3.4 18 MM DEEP
B. 3.4 THROUGH HOLE   QUANTITY 2 OFF
-----CUT INTO TWO PIECES AS SHOWN DOTTED-----
HOLES (AFTER SPLITTING)
A. 5/32" X 40 ME
B. 5/32" X 40 ME
C. 4.5 2 MM DEEP
D. 4.5 THROUGH HOLE

CLAMP BODY C1

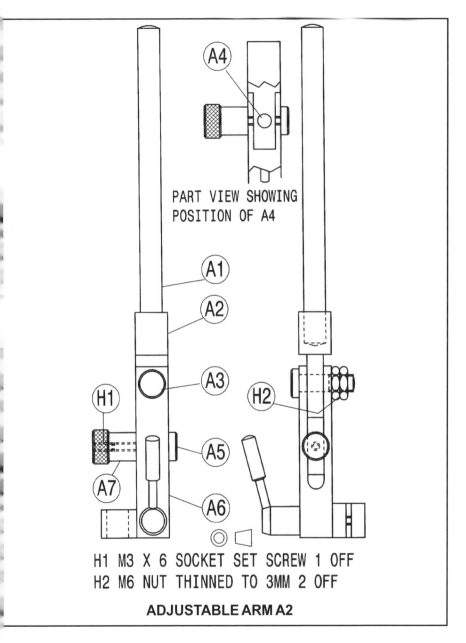

PART VIEW SHOWING
POSITION OF A4

H1 M3 X 6 SOCKET SET SCREW 1 OFF
H2 M6 NUT THINNED TO 3MM 2 OFF

ADJUSTABLE ARM A2

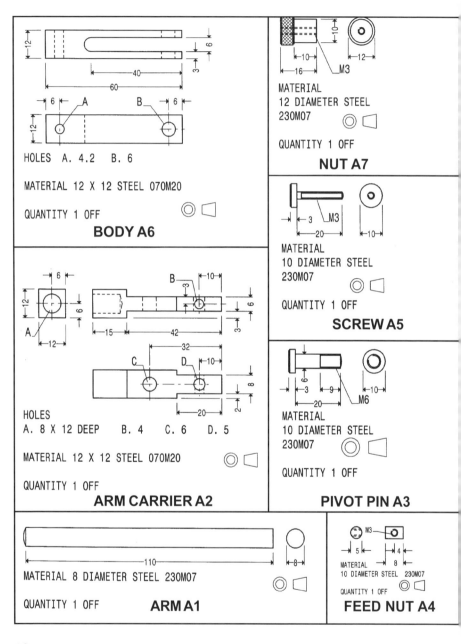

HOLES A. 4.2   B. 6

MATERIAL 12 X 12 STEEL 070M20

QUANTITY 1 OFF

BODY A6

MATERIAL
12 DIAMETER STEEL
230M07

QUANTITY 1 OFF

NUT A7

MATERIAL
10 DIAMETER STEEL
230M07

QUANTITY 1 OFF

SCREW A5

HOLES
A. 8 X 12 DEEP   B. 4   C. 6   D. 5

MATERIAL 12 X 12 STEEL 070M20

QUANTITY 1 OFF

ARM CARRIER A2

MATERIAL
10 DIAMETER STEEL
230M07

QUANTITY 1 OFF

PIVOT PIN A3

MATERIAL 8 DIAMETER STEEL 230M07

QUANTITY 1 OFF   ## ARM A1

MATERIAL
10 DIAMETER STEEL   230M07

QUANTITY 1 OFF

FEED NUT A4

Chapter 13

Faceplate Balancing Fixture

Having fixed your workpiece in the correct position on the lathe's faceplate it is still essential to balance the assembly by the addition of suitably placed weights. This is necessary else it will often be impossible to run the lathe at the speed required. Accurate balancing will certainly be necessary where the operation requires the lathe to run at a high speed.

Whilst balancing can be carried out on the lathe, the drag on the bearings and the problem of keeping the belts clear of

Photo 1 The finished faceplate balancing fixture.

Right: Photo 2 In the vertical position as used for balancing.

Right: Photo 3 Placed in the horizontal position, loading the faceplate is much more easy than whilst mounted on the lathe.

Photo 4 The parts that make up the fixture.

the pulleys can make it difficult to achieve. To overcome this problem, the bearings in this fixture are free running, making it possible to achieve a near perfect balance. As an indication of how free running the assembly is, the prototype runs for 25 seconds when fitted with an empty faceplate and given a rapid spin.

Photo 1 shows the completed fixture with **Photo 2** showing it in the normal working position for balancing. However, the fixture has another feature that is that the faceplate can be swung into the horizontal position for loading the workpiece, **Photo 3**. In this arrangement fitting the workpiece is much easier as gravity is helping, rather than hindering as it does when mounted to the lathe's spindle. With some workpieces a DTI could also be mounted off the fixtures

bracket and then used to position the workpiece precisely as Photo 3 illustrates.

The design achieves its free running ability by incorporating shop made bearings using 4mm balls. These can be obtained cheaply from your local cycle repair shop.

Most parts required are easy to make and need no comment but for others concentricity is vital. The following give a very brief idea how this can be achieved but does not though detail the complete manufacturing process. Do also study carefully the spindle assembly drawing so that you are fully aware of the requirements in terms of accuracy, concentricity, etc. Also, the spindle nose is dimensioned to suit a Myford Series Seven lathe, for other lathes you will no doubt have to change some dimensions

Spindle (3)

The important requirements for this are that, the face plate mounting, the angled surface of the bearing and the 14mm diameter on which the end bearing is mounted are all concentric. Ideally, to achieve this, the part should be machined between centres. The prototype also has a Morse taper socket though I have never found this to be of use. Because of this I have not included it on the drawings, if however you wish to include this it places additional complications in terms of machining the spindle

End bearing (8)

Concentricity of the angled bearing surface and the 14mm bore are the essential features and machining them at the same visit to the lathe will ensure this. The bore must also be a very close fit on the spindle.

Outer Bearing (4)

This is probably the most complex as the two bores that need to be concentric are at opposite ends of the component. Bore one end but do not produce the through bore of 30mm diameter. Remove from the chuck, turn and refit, and bore the other end 28mm diameter 25mm deep, drill through 8.5mm diameter, remove from the chuck

Mount a short piece of 50mm steel in the chuck and make a stub mandrel a very close fit in the 40mm bore already made and long enough so that the end of the mandrel, suitably faced, contacts the base of the bore. Do not remove the mandrel

from the chuck but drill and tap M8. The outer bearing can now be fitted to this and the 40mm bore on the second end made. This process will ensure the two bores are concentric and their bases parallel. Remove from the mandrel and refit into the chuck and through bore as per drawing.

Photo 4 shows all the parts prior to final assembly. Incidentally, the Angle (10) can easily be removed and with this done it may find other uses, on the milling machine maybe.

Of all the items in this book, this one improves the task being undertaken by more than any other, only the faceplate clamps, Chapter 9 coming close.

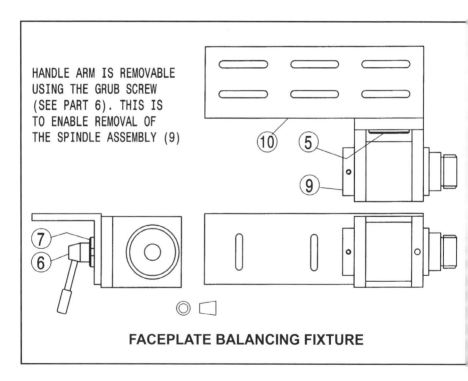

HANDLE ARM IS REMOVABLE USING THE GRUB SCREW (SEE PART 6). THIS IS TO ENABLE REMOVAL OF THE SPINDLE ASSEMBLY (9)

FACEPLATE BALANCING FIXTURE

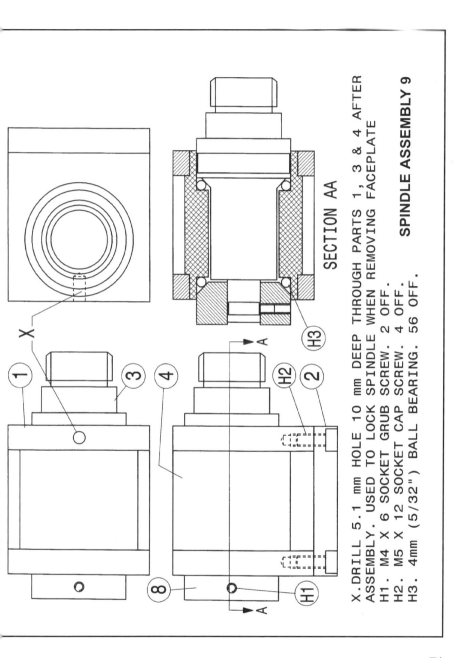

SECTION AA

SPINDLE ASSEMBLY 9

X. DRILL 5.1 mm HOLE 10 mm DEEP THROUGH PARTS 1, 3 & 4 AFTER
ASSEMBLY. USED TO LOCK SPINDLE WHEN REMOVING FACEPLATE
H1. M4 X 6 SOCKET GRUB SCREW. 2 OFF.
H2. M5 X 12 SOCKET CAP SCREW. 4 OFF.
H3. 4mm (5/32") BALL BEARING. 56 OFF.

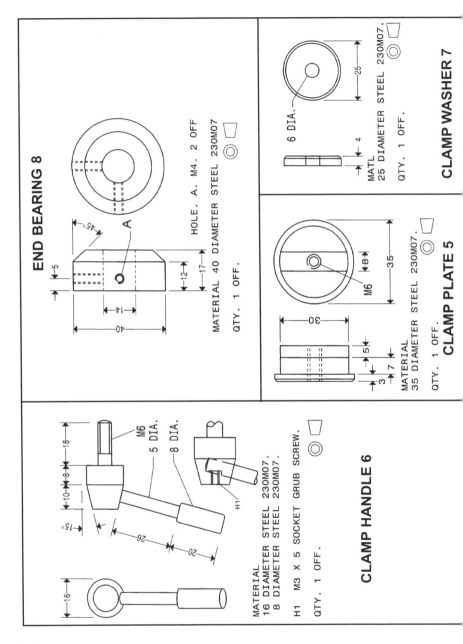

END BEARING 8

A

HOLE. A. M4. 2 OFF

MATERIAL 40 DIAMETER STEEL 230M07

QTY. 1 OFF.

CLAMP WASHER 7

6 DIA.

MATL
25 DIAMETER STEEL 230M07.

QTY. 1 OFF.

CLAMP PLATE 5

M6

MATERIAL
35 DIAMETER STEEL 230M07.

QTY. 1 OFF.

CLAMP HANDLE 6

M6

5 DIA.

8 DIA.

H1

MATERIAL
16 DIAMETER STEEL 230M07.
8 DIAMETER STEEL 230M07.

H1 M3 X 5 SOCKET GRUB SCREW.

QTY. 1 OFF.

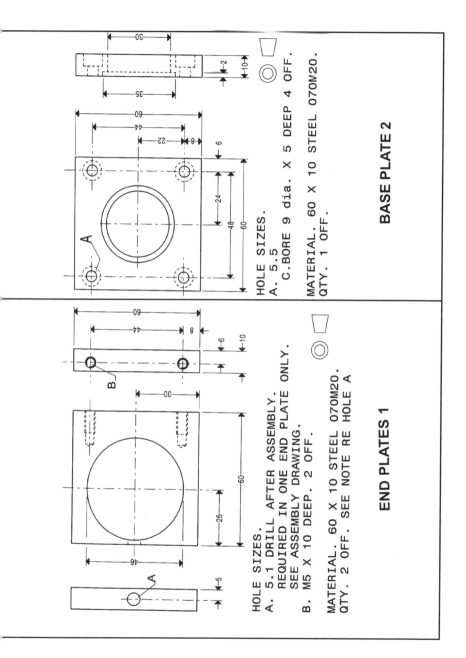

BASE PLATE 2

HOLE SIZES.
A. 5.5
   C.BORE 9 dia. X 5 DEEP 4 OFF.

MATERIAL. 60 X 10 STEEL 070M20.
QTY. 1 OFF.

END PLATES 1

HOLE SIZES.
A. 5.1 DRILL AFTER ASSEMBLY.
   REQUIRED IN ONE END PLATE ONLY.
   SEE ASSEMBLY DRAWING.
B. M5 X 10 DEEP. 2 OFF.

MATERIAL. 60 X 10 STEEL 070M20.
QTY. 2 OFF. SEE NOTE RE HOLE A

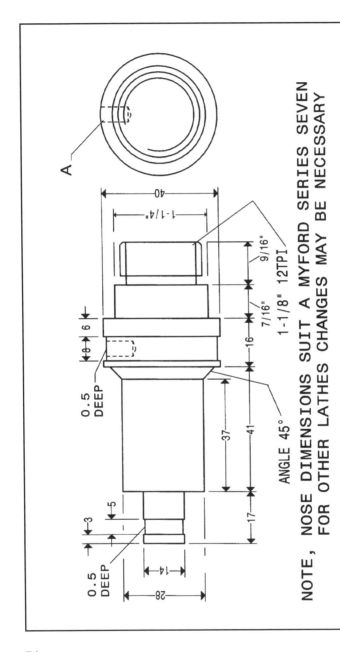

A

40

1-1/4"

9/16"

1-1/8" 12TPI

7/16"

16

ANGLE 45°

6

8

0.5 DEEP

37

41

17

5

3

0.5 DEEP

14

28

NOTE, NOSE DIMENSIONS SUIT A MYFORD SERIES SEVEN FOR OTHER LATHES CHANGES MAY BE NECESSARY

HOLE SIZES. A. 5.1. DRILL AFTER ASSEMBLY WITH END PLATE AND BEARING.

MATERIAL. 40 DIAMETER STEEL 230M07.   QTY. 1 OFF.

SPINDLE 3

74

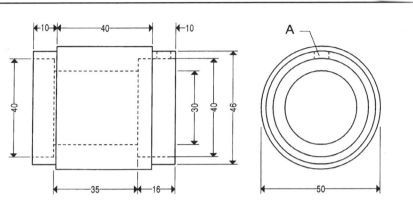

HOLE SIZES. A. 5.1 DRILL AFTER ASSEMBLY WITH
END PLATE AND SPINDLE.

MATERIAL. 5O DIAMETER STEEL 230MO7.
QTY. 1 OFF.

OUTER BEARING 4

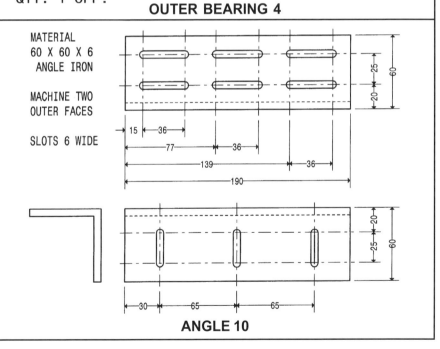

MATERIAL
60 X 60 X 6
ANGLE IRON

MACHINE TWO
OUTER FACES

SLOTS 6 WIDE

ANGLE 10

Chapter 14

Low Profile Clamps

Whilst other clamping methods will find much more use on the milling machine, the clamps in this chapter will make some tasks possible which would otherwise be almost impossible. **Photo 1** shows a piece of black iron that was too large for the available vice having its upper face surfaced.

Even though the clamps are referred to as "low profile" as the clamping action is close to the machine's table; they can be used with much thicker materials providing the necessary precautions are taken.

1. Most important is, that once the height of the component becomes more than a few millimetres higher than the clamp itself then the component's foot print on the machine table must be appreciably longer than its height. Typically, if machining at 40mm above the worktable then a workpiece length of 100mm should be considered a minimum.

2. Never use less than two clamps, preferably more when machining well above the worktable.

3. Always limit the cutting depth/feed when working well above the machine table.

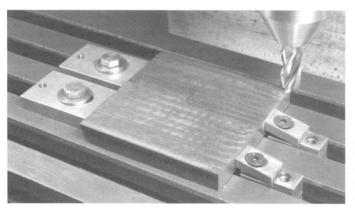

Photo 1 Type four clamps being used to hold a piece of black iron for surfacing.

Photo 2 The five types of clamps, type's one to five left to right.

Having made those comments it is worth bearing in mind that a higher fixed jaw will help considerably.

With these precautions being observed then the clamps will be found to be a very valuable addition to one's workshop equipment

The clamps

The common feature of all five clamps, **Photo 2**, described is the method in which they are held in position. Reference to the assembly drawings will show that each have a grub screw (H1). This is used to firmly locate the clamp in place by tightening the screw down into the base of the tee slot. In other respects each clamp uses a different approach to providing the clamping action. The five assembly drawings should make this clear.

Clamp three has the advantage of being far the easiest to make and works well but with one limitation, that is, it can only clamp surfaces that are at nominally right angles to the tee slot. Clamps 4 and 5 have the same limitation but have the advantage that the clamping action tends to hold the workpiece against the worktable as well as the fixed jaw. Clamp 4 is particularly good in this respect.

Clamps 1 and 2 do though have the advantage of being able to hold non-rectangular workpieces due to them both having rotating jaws. If though the workpiece has one straight edge it maybe that the fixed jaws can accommodate the irregular shape in which case clamps 3, 4 and 5 may be in with a chance

If all things considered you decide not to make any of the clamps detailed then clamps rather similar to clamp 1 are to be had commercially

I doubt if many readers will wish to make all five types but would suggest that you make a minimum of four clamps. If you wish to experiment then you could make more than one type. In this case I would though recommend a minimum of

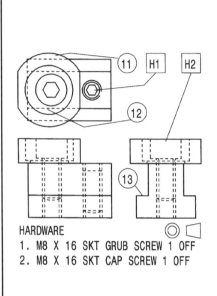

HARDWARE
1. M8 X 16 SKT GRUB SCREW 1 OFF
2. M8 X 16 SKT CAP SCREW 1 OFF

CLAMP ASSEMBLY 1

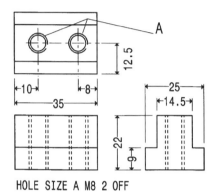

HOLE SIZE A M8 2 OFF

MATERIAL 25 SQ. STEEL 230M07

QUANTITY 1 OFF PER CLAMP

T NUT 13

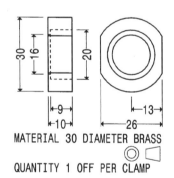

MATERIAL 30 DIAMETER BRASS

QUANTITY 1 OFF PER CLAMP

CLAMP PIECE 11

MATERIAL
20 DIAMETER STEEL 230M07

QUANTITY 1 PER CLAMP

CAM 12

two of each type made.

The dimensions suit a 16mm wide tee slot you will need to change at least some dimensions for other slot sizes

One point that is not covered on the drawings is that for clamp 1 the screw (H2) is to be fitted into the cam (12) using a two-part resin adhesive. If you would like to be a little more confident regarding this you could drill across the joint between the outer diameter of the screw head and the inner diameter of the cam and fit a close fitting pin, again held with adhesive.

In use

Using the clamps is straightforward but you only need to use the clamps on one side of the part being held. On the other side a fixed jaw, or jaws, should be provided which must be firmly clamped with a through screw. Do not use an overhead clamp to hold the jaw as the clamping pressure can be quite large in which case the fixed jaw may move.

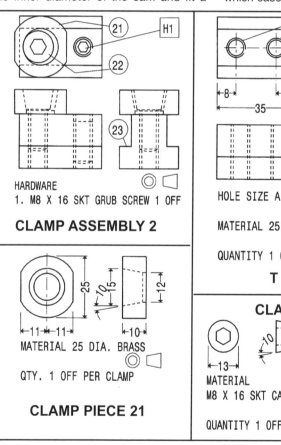

HARDWARE
1. M8 X 16 SKT GRUB SCREW 1 OFF

CLAMP ASSEMBLY 2

MATERIAL 25 DIA. BRASS

QTY. 1 OFF PER CLAMP

CLAMP PIECE 21

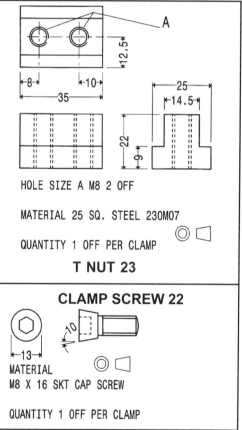

HOLE SIZE A M8 2 OFF

MATERIAL 25 SQ. STEEL 230M07

QUANTITY 1 OFF PER CLAMP

T NUT 23

CLAMP SCREW 22

MATERIAL
M8 X 16 SKT CAP SCREW

QUANTITY 1 OFF PER CLAMP

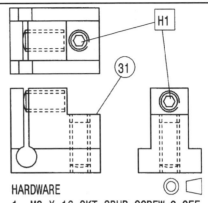

HARDWARE
1. M8 X 16 SKT GRUB SCREW 2 OFF

CLAMP ASSEMBLY 3

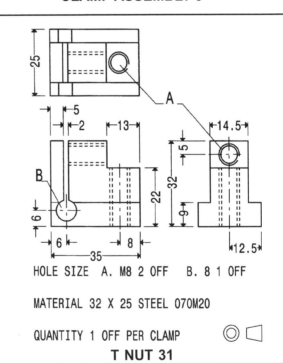

HOLE SIZE   A. M8 2 OFF   B. 8 1 OFF

MATERIAL 32 X 25 STEEL 070M20

QUANTITY 1 OFF PER CLAMP

T NUT 31

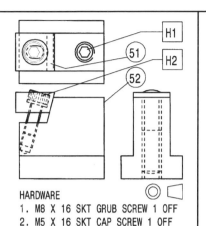

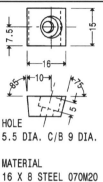

HARDWARE
1. M8 X 16 SKT GRUB SCREW 1 OFF
2. M5 X 16 SKT CAP SCREW 1 OFF

CLAMP ASSEMBLY 4

HOLE
5.5 DIA. C/B 9 DIA.

MATERIAL
16 X 8 STEEL 070M20

QUANTITY
1 OFF PER CLAMP

CLAMP 41

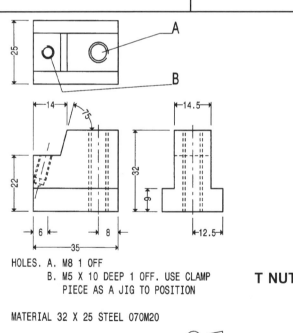

HOLES. A. M8 1 OFF
B. M5 X 10 DEEP 1 OFF. USE CLAMP
PIECE AS A JIG TO POSITION

T NUT 42

MATERIAL 32 X 25 STEEL 070M20

QUANTITY 1 OFF PER CLAMP

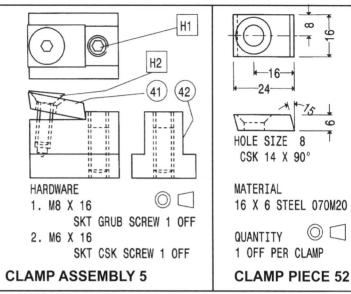

HARDWARE
1. M8 X 16
   SKT GRUB SCREW 1 OFF
2. M6 X 16
   SKT CSK SCREW 1 OFF

CLAMP ASSEMBLY 5

HOLE SIZE 8
CSK 14 X 90°

MATERIAL
16 X 6 STEEL 070M20

QUANTITY
1 OFF PER CLAMP

CLAMP PIECE 52

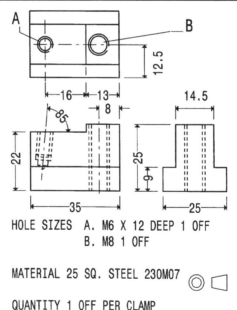

HOLE SIZES A. M6 X 12 DEEP 1 OFF
            B. M8 1 OFF

MATERIAL 25 SQ. STEEL 230M07

QUANTITY 1 OFF PER CLAMP

T NUT 52

Chapter 15

Engineers Sash Clamps

Sash clamps, or should that be cramps, are in commercial terms a product for the cabinetmaker. However, I decided that a smaller, but more robust, version could be of use in the engineer's workshop and the result is seen in **Photo 1**.

Since having made these their use has mostly been as a milling machine table vice for large items, a task that they perform well as seen in **Photos 2** and **3**. However, they are not limited to this task as **Photo 4** shows. In this, the two ends of the head assembly for the tapping stand, Chapter 16, are being held together whilst the adhesive sets.

Manufacture is straightforward other than to say that the holes along the length of the bar must be equally spaced. In terms

Photo 1 The finished clamps, do make at least two.

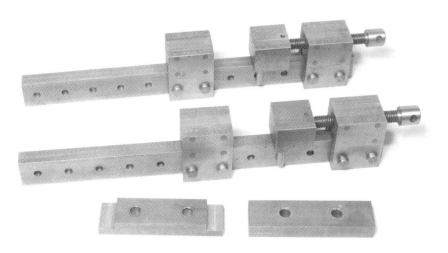

of length you may like to make the clamps longer by a few more pitches as I have found that this would have been useful on a number of occasions.

The two bars as seen at the front of Photo 1 are for securing the clamps onto the milling machine table as seen in Photo 2. I have not drawn and dimensioned these, as they need to be made to suit, in particular the pitch of the holes to match the spacing of the tee slots on your machine

Above: Photo 2 Being used to hold a large flat plate.

Right: Photo 3 Being used to hold a large casting.

Photo 4 *Use is not confined solely to the milling machine. In this case three parts are being held whilst the adhesive being used sets. See Head Assembly Chapter 16.*

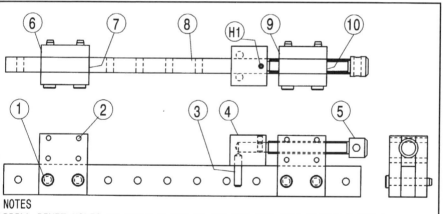

NOTES
DRILL RIVET HOLES IN PARTS 7 AND 10 AND ONE OFF SIDE PLATES 6 AND 9
ON ASSEMBLY. USE PINS 1 AND BAR 8 TO ALIGN PARTS

THE QUANTITIES ON THE PART DRAWINGS ARE FOR ONE CLAMP ONLY. IT IS SUGGESTED
THAT TWO CLAMPS SHOULD BE MADE FOR USE IN PAIRS AS A MACHINE VICE.

HARDWARE H1 M4x6 SOCKET GRUB SCREW   **ENGINEERS SASH CLAMP**

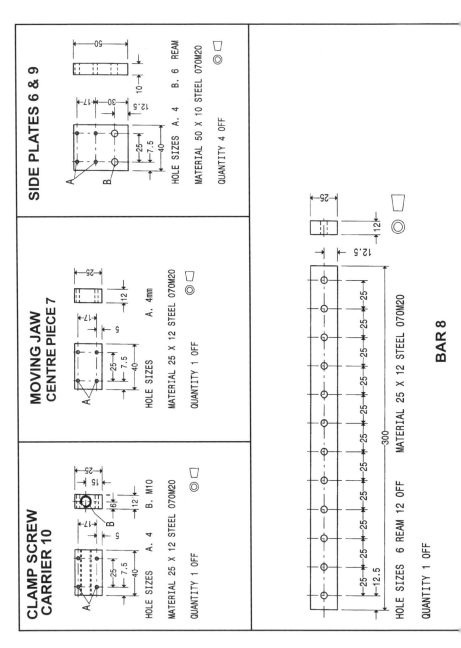

SIDE PLATES 6 & 9

HOLE SIZES   A. 4   B. 6   REAM

MATERIAL 50 X 10 STEEL 070M20

QUANTITY 4 OFF

MOVING JAW CENTRE PIECE 7

HOLE SIZES   A. 4mm

MATERIAL 25 X 12 STEEL 070M20

QUANTITY 1 OFF

CLAMP SCREW CARRIER 10

HOLE SIZES   A. 4   B. M10

MATERIAL 25 X 12 STEEL 070M20

QUANTITY 1 OFF

BAR 8

HOLE SIZES 6 REAM 12 OFF   MATERIAL 25 X 12 STEEL 070M20

QUANTITY 1 OFF

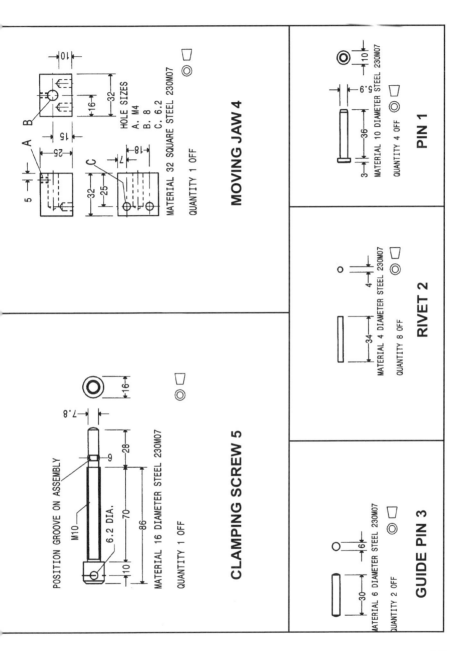

HOLE SIZES
A. M4
B. 8
C. 6.2

MATERIAL 32 SQUARE STEEL 230M07

QUANTITY 1 OFF

MOVING JAW 4

MATERIAL 10 DIAMETER STEEL 230M07

QUANTITY 4 OFF

PIN 1

MATERIAL 4 DIAMETER STEEL 230M07

QUANTITY 8 OFF

RIVET 2

POSITION GROOVE ON ASSEMBLY

M10

6.2 DIA.

MATERIAL 16 DIAMETER STEEL 230M07

QUANTITY 1 OFF

CLAMPING SCREW 5

MATERIAL 6 DIAMETER STEEL 230M07

QUANTITY 2 OFF

GUIDE PIN 3

Chapter 16

Tapping Stand

Whilst the tapping guides described in Chapter 2 will be of considerable benefit for many applications, the tapping stand here has some very worthwhile advantages. The major feature of the stand, **Photo 1**, is that the tap is automatically fed at the pitch of the thread being cut. In simple terms, this means that the tap only needs turning as the stand will feed the tap into the workpiece.

The main advantage of this is that there is no need to use a taper tap, as a plug tap will start the thread perfectly adequately. This particularly makes it a simple operation to tap shallow blind holes a task that is otherwise difficult due to it not being possible to use a taper tap. Not only does it achieve this aim but also it does it perfectly, no partial threads at the commencement of the hole, as there would likely be if hand tapped using a plug tap only.

Another advantage is its ability to accurately start a thread into a non-flat surface where the simple guides would be of no help. **Photo 2** shows a typical example. In this case, one of the tailstock die holders featured in Chapter 8 is seen being tapped.

For one or two holes into a flat surface then using the simple guides will be more than adequate. However, for more holes

Photo 1 The complete Tapping Stand.

88

Photo 2 Being used to tap into a curved surface where the simple guides in Chapter 2 would be of no use.

screw will be required. The self-feed can though be overridden if a one off special pitch thread for which you have not made a feed screw assembly surfaces.

To gain most benefit from using the stand, or any other hand tapping for that matter, do carefully choose the tapping drill size used. Unfortunately, most charts do not quote the resulting thread depth and in most cases quote a drill that is unnecessarily small. A thread depth of between 60 and 70 % depth will be more than adequate for all but the most demanding applications. It will also reduce appreciably the likelihood of a broken tap.

Manufacture

Manufacture is easy, only concentricity being important with the feed screw components (7 and 8) tap holder (11) and the tap carrier (10). With the later, the bores at both ends must be concentric and this will need the bore at one end to be made whilst the part is held on a stub mandrel at the other

The feed screws do not need to be a close fit in the thread in the tap carrier spindle (8). In fact, a loose fitting thread will give some leeway in terms of concentricity. Because of this the design proposes using off the shelf screws for use as the feed screw

Using

In use, operation is straightforward. However, for larger threads and or smaller components, a vice to hold the workpiece should be used. For larger threads, say M6, then the component should be firmly

or into more difficult locations, than the stand is a joy to use.

Photo 3 shows the parts that provide the main feature, that is the auto feed, with **Photo 4** showing the feed screw for one pitch in close up. The feed screw though does not have to have the same pitch and diameter as the thread being tapped, only the pitch being important. Typically therefor, if you use a lot of 40 TPI model engineer threads, only one 40 TPI feed

Photo 3 The feed screw mechanisms for threads M3 to M8 together with the taps already in their holders.

clamped to the table allowing both hands to be used to turn the tap. The slotted table makes this easy but you may even like to make some tee nuts to make this even easier than using just nuts and washers.

A final comment

Having arrived at the book's end I do hope you have been able to make some of the items illustrated and found them as useful as I have!

Photo 4 The M6 feed screw mechanism in close up.

TAPPING STAND

HARDWARE
H1 M5 X 8 SOCKET GRUB SCREW 2 OFF
H2 M5 X 25 SOCKET CAP SCREW 4 OFF
H3 M4 X 12 SOCKET CAP SCREW 10 OFF
H4 FEED SCREW
   DIAMETER AND LENGTH TO SUIT PITCH
H5 M4 X 6 SOCKET GRUB SCREW 1 OFF
H6 M3 X 4 SOCKET GRUB SCREW
      4 OFF PER TAP HOLDER(11)
H7 M4 X 10 SOCKET CAP SCREW 1 OFF

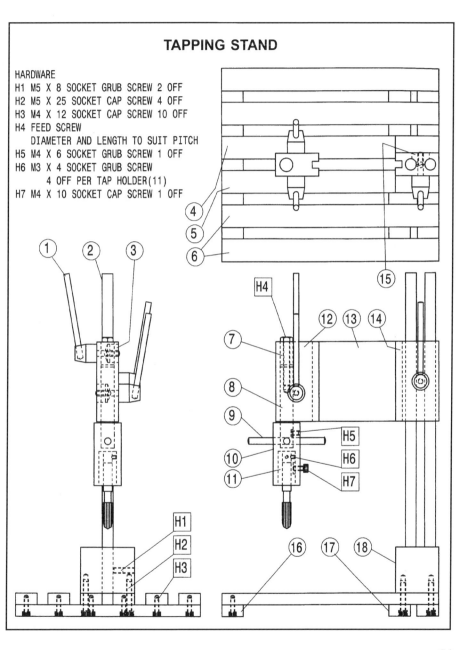

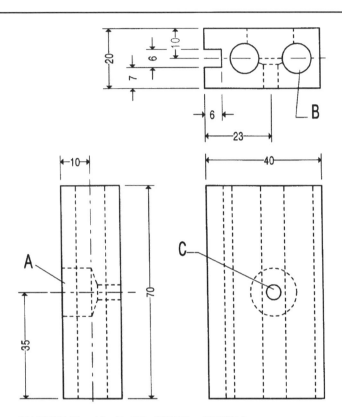

MATERIAL 40 X 20 STEEL 070M20

DRILL HOLES B AFTER ASSEMBLY WITH PARTS
3,15, 12 AND 13 NOTING DIMENSIONS ON
HEAD ASSEMBLY DRAWING.

HOLES   A. 16   B. 10   2 OFF   C. 5.2

QUANTITY 1 OFF

COLUMN BRACKET 14

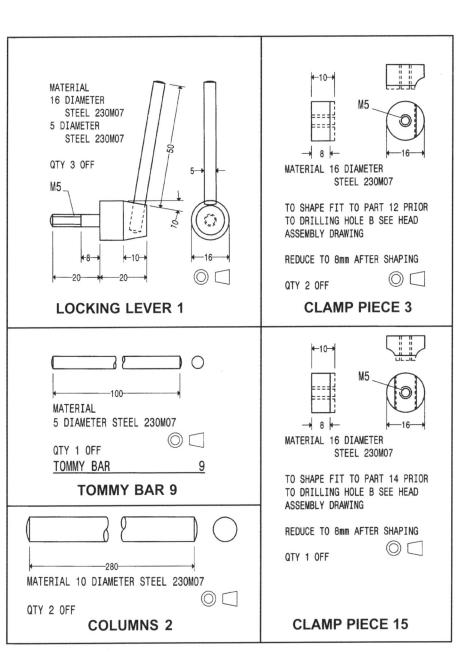

MATERIAL
16 DIAMETER
   STEEL 230M07
5 DIAMETER
   STEEL 230M07

QTY 3 OFF

M5

50

5

10

M5

8

10

16

20

20

LOCKING LEVER 1

MATERIAL
5 DIAMETER STEEL 230M07

QTY 1 OFF

TOMMY BAR   9

100

TOMMY BAR 9

280

MATERIAL 10 DIAMETER STEEL 230M07

QTY 2 OFF

COLUMNS 2

10

M5

8

16

MATERIAL 16 DIAMETER
    STEEL 230M07

TO SHAPE FIT TO PART 12 PRIOR
TO DRILLING HOLE B SEE HEAD
ASSEMBLY DRAWING

REDUCE TO 8mm AFTER SHAPING

QTY 2 OFF

CLAMP PIECE 3

10

M5

8

16

MATERIAL 16 DIAMETER
    STEEL 230M07

TO SHAPE FIT TO PART 14 PRIOR
TO DRILLING HOLE B SEE HEAD
ASSEMBLY DRAWING

REDUCE TO 8mm AFTER SHAPING

QTY 1 OFF

CLAMP PIECE 15

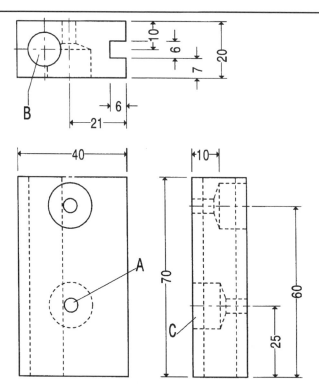

MATERIAL 40 X 20 STEEL 070M20

DRILL HOLE B AFTER ASSEMBLY WITH PARTS
3, 15, 13 AND 14 NOTING DIMENSIONS ON
HEAD ASSEMBLY DRAWING.

HOLE SIZES
A. 5.2 2 OFF B. 12 1 OFF C. 16 2 OFF

QUANTITY 1 OFF

SPINDLE BEARING BLOCK 12

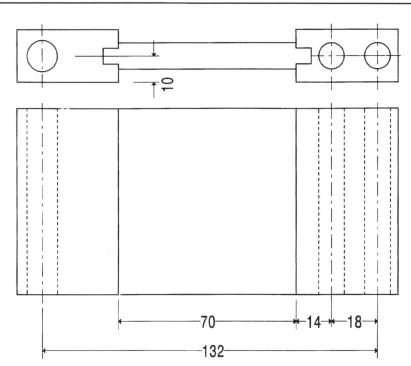

ASSEMBLE HEAD, PARTS 12, 13 AND 14, USING TWO
PART RESIN ADHESIVE
TO ENSURE HOLES ARE PARALLEL DO NOT REMOVE
FROM THE VICE OR ANGLE PLATE BETWEEN
DRILLING HOLES B

HEAD ASSEMBLY

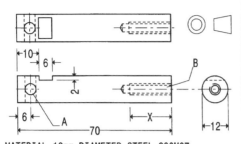

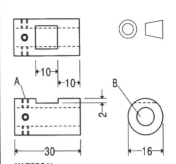

<10> 6

B

2

6

A

X

70

12

MATERIAL 12mm DIAMETER STEEL 230M07

HOLE A. 5.2mm 2 OFF
    B. AS THREAD IN FEED SCREW CARRIER.
MUST BE CONCENTRIC WITH 12mm OUTSIDE
DIAMETER.
DEPTH "X" DEPENDENT ON THREAD SIZE
TYPICALLY 15mm FOR M3 AND 25mm FOR M8

QUANTITY 1 OFF FOR EACH FEED SCREW PITCH

USE TAP CARRIER AS A JIG TO DRILL HOLES A.

TAP CARRIER SPINDLE 8

A
<10> <10>
B
2
30
16

MATERIAL
16mm DIAMETER STEEL 230M07

HOLE A. M3 4 OFF
    B. TAP SHANK DIAMETER PLUS
0.1mm/0.2mm. MUST BE CONCENTRIC
WITH 16mm OUTSIDE DIAMETER.

QUANTITY 1 OFF FOR EACH
TAP DIAMETER

TAP HOLDER 11

20   12

MATERIAL
12mm DIAMETER STEEL 230M07

HOLE TO SUIT PITCH REQUIRED

QUANTITY 1 OFF FOR EACH PITCH.

NOTE, THREAD DIAMETER DOES NOT
HAVE TO BE THE SAME AS THE
THREAD BEING MADE
TAPPED HOLE MUST BE CONCENTRIC
WITH THE 12mm OUTER DIAMETER.

FEED SCREW CARRIER 7

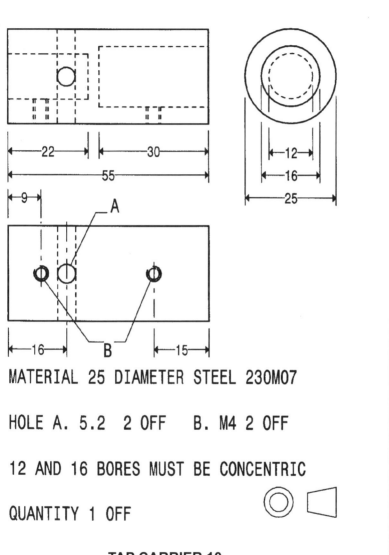

MATERIAL 25 DIAMETER STEEL 230M07

HOLE A. 5.2   2 OFF   B. M4 2 OFF

12 AND 16 BORES MUST BE CONCENTRIC

QUANTITY 1 OFF

TAP CARRIER 10

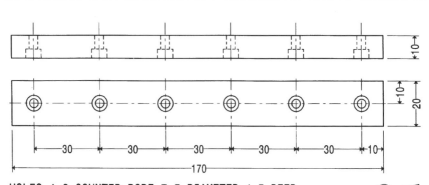

HOLES 4.2 COUNTER BORE 7.5 DIAMETER 4.5 DEEP

MATERIAL 20 X 10 STEEL 070M20 QUANTITY 1 OFF

REAR BARS 16

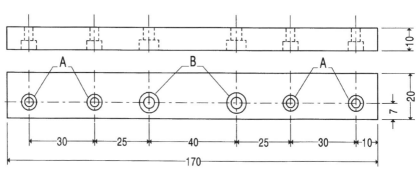

HOLES A. 4.2 COUNTER BORE 7.5 DIAMETER 4.5 DEEP
B. 5.2 COUNTER BORE 9 DIAMETER 5.5 DEEP

MATERIAL 20 X 10 STEEL 070M20   QUANTITY 2 OFF

REAR BARS 17

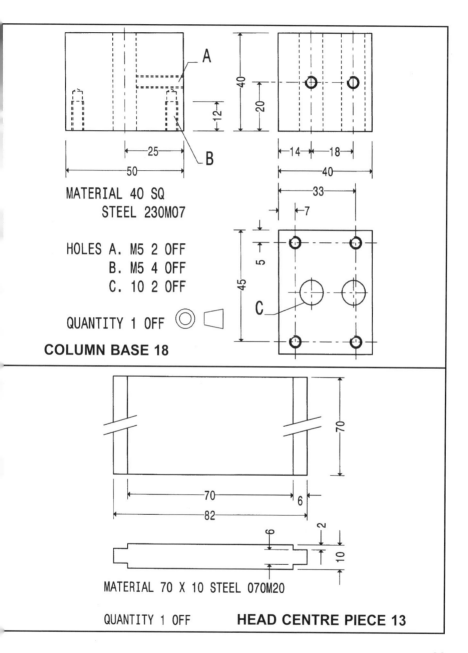

A

B

MATERIAL 40 SQ
STEEL 230M07

HOLES A. M5 2 OFF
B. M5 4 OFF
C. 10 2 OFF

QUANTITY 1 OFF

COLUMN BASE 18

C

MATERIAL 70 X 10 STEEL 070M20

QUANTITY 1 OFF   **HEAD CENTRE PIECE 13**

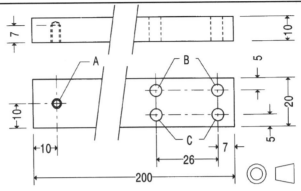

HOLES A. M4
        B. 5.2 2 OFF DRILL IN PART 4 ONLY
        C. 5.2 2 OFF DRILL IN PART 5 ONLY

MATERIAL 20 X 10 STEEL 070M20

QUANTITY 1 OFF PART 4 1 OFF PART 5

CENTRE BARS 4 & 5

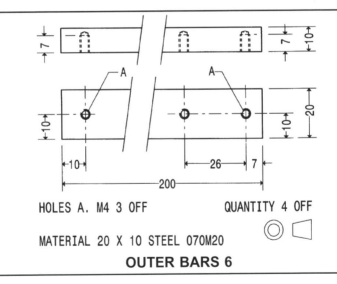

HOLES A. M4 3 OFF   QUANTITY 4 OFF

MATERIAL 20 X 10 STEEL 070M20

OUTER BARS 6